Hitler

and

The Screaming Eagles

Born in York, Charles Whiting, who writes as Leo Kessler inter alia, has now had over 200 books published, encompassing action fiction, military history, espionage and biography.

Hitler's Lair

and

The Screaming Eagles

Leo Kessler

Pan Books

Hitler's Lair first published 1999 by Severn House Publishers
as *Battle for Hitler's Eagle's Nest*
The Screaming Eagles first published 1983 by Arrow Books
under the pseudonym Duncan Stirling

This omnibus edition published 2001 by Pan Books
an imprint of Pan Macmillan Ltd
Pan Macmillan, 20 New Wharf Road, London N1 9RR
Basingstoke and Oxford
Associated companies throughout the world
www.panmacmillan.com

ISBN 0 330 39881 4

1 3 5 7 9 8 6 4 2

A CIP catalogue record for this book is available from
the British Library.

Printed and bound in Great Britain by
Mackays of Chatham plc, Chatham, Kent

Hitler's Lair

"[It is] an observatory floating in space, perched like an eagle's nest, a castle of the Grail."

Andre Francois-Poncet,
French Ambassador to Nazi Germany, 1934

Part One
Flight from Berlin

"I swear to you, Adolf Hitler, as Führer and Reich Chancellor, my undivided loyalty and bravery. I vow to you and to those whom you name to command me, my obedience unto death. So help me God."

SS Assault Regiment Wotan
Oath of Allegiance

One

"Sir," the dying man said, looking up at von Dodenburg, "we've had it, haven't we?" He looked down at his stomach. The shell fragment had ripped a huge hole in it. From the bloody torn gap, his guts were sliding like a monstrous, smoking, large grey snake. On the debris-littered pavement where he lay there were thick red splotches of blood everywhere.

Obersturmbannführer von Dodenburg, the last commander of SS Assault Regiment Wotan, wiped the sweat from his brow. He threw a look at the dying man and then at the Ivan positions further down the *Ku-Damm*. The Russian attackers had gone to ground again. Their last assault had failed miserably. The SS had mowed them down mercilessly. The bodies of the Ivan dead in their padded grey tunics lay everywhere in gutters and smoking piles of brick rubble. But they'd attack again. Von Dodenburg knew that. Their political commissars would be giving them the usual pep talks at that very moment. The *politruks* would be urging them to new efforts, promising reinforcements, medals, mass rape, and firing up the soldiers' flagging spirits with plenty of strong vodka.

He ducked instinctively as a burst of machine-gun fire zipped across the fifty odd metres separating the two fronts.

"Arses with ears," big hulking Sergeant-Major Schulze, crouching next to him, cursed routinely. It seemed as if he hadn't the energy to get angry any more; they'd all been fighting for Berlin for too long. They were at the end of their tethers. The tall SS Colonel, his face hollowed out to a scarlet

3

death's head in the lurid flame coming from the burning gas jet opposite, knew that all right. One more attack by the Ivans and that would be it. His men of Wotan, old hares and greenhorns alike, would break.

Sprawled on the pavement, the dying man groaned, caught himself and said in the hoarse whisper of those who aren't much longer for this world, "We, we tried our best, Sir . . . didn't we?" He coughed. A thin trickle of dark red blood seeped from the corner of his lips. "Sorry I bought one . . . let you down like this."

Von Dodenburg fought back his tears. The dying man was not much older than seventeen. He'd come up only hours before as a replacement. God in Heaven, he didn't even know the kid's name. Now he had led him to his death and the kid was somehow apologising to him. *For dying!* Heaven, arse and cloudburst, it was nearly too much for a man to bear.

"They're coming out for another polka, sir," Matz, another old hare, dug in a few metres in front of the others, called over his shoulder, not taking his eyes off the battle-littered street for one instant.

"All right, arse-with-ears," Schulze, his old comrade sneered, "don't fill yer knickers. We can see 'em as well, y'know." He slapped another magazine into his machine pistol and clasped it at the ready in his massive fists; the weapon looked like a kid's toy.

A little helplessly, von Dodenburg looked down at the dying SS man. In the last few moments, his face seemed to have sunk. His eyes stared out, large and intense, from those pinched features which von Dodenburg had seen all too often on battlefields over three continents in these last five terrible years.

"I don't want to fall into their hands, sir," the boy quavered, fear lending energy to his words. "You know what they do to us from Wotan, if they capture us . . . alive . . . Better if . . ." He didn't complete the sentence, but von Dodenburg knew well enough what he meant.

In Karkov, Russia, back in '43 when the Regiment had lost

and recaptured the key city, they had found scores of their
own men, who had been left behind wounded, stuffed down
wells and pit shafts, with grenades thrown in to slaughter them
en masse. Since then, SS Assault Regiment Wotan had always
dealt – even mentally he couldn't make himself use the real
word – with seriously wounded casualties in their own fashion.
Obviously, the boy without a name knew that, too. For he was
looking up at the CO, his young life ebbing away rapidly, with
a look of almost pleading in his eyes.

"*Gunner!*" Schulze yelled urgently, cutting into von Dodenburg's thoughts, "get that frigging Hitler Saw working, man!
Or do yer want a frigging invite?"

The gunner turned his "Hitler Saw", otherwise known as
the German Army's MG 42, round in the direction of the first
Ivans emerging from the ruins on their right flank. Without
taking aim, he pressed the trigger. The machine gun burst into
frenetic activity. Tracer sliced the air lethally, the Russians
caught by surprise. It was as if they were jerking marionettes in
the hands of a puppet master suddenly gone mad. They fell to
all sides, twitching and screaming, their limbs jolting at impossible angles, writhing and squirming in their death throes.
In an instant it was all over. The survivors fled back the way
they had come, with their wounded hobbling and pleading,
staggering behind them, as the Russian mortars opened up
with an obscene howl. Next moment and the mortar bombs
began exploding, flooding the SS positions at the end of
Berlin's once most fashionable street. Time was now beginning to run out fast.

Von Dodenburg cowered, pistol in hand, mind racing
electrically, as the red-hot slivers of steel hissed lethally left
and right. The shrapnel twanged and howled off the ruined
buildings. Here and there more gas mains exploded. House
walls swayed and trembled like stage sets caught in a sudden
wind. Everything was confusion and chaos. On the pavement,
the dying Wotan trooper fought back his moans. Slowly,
painfully slowly, he caught his guts in his hands, cradling
them like a loving mother might a dear child.

"Sir," he said brokenly, "can you do . . . it . . . now?" The words came out in staccato jerks. "Please . . . sir . . ." He looked up at von Dodenburg, his eyes liquid with agony.

Crouched behind the CO, Schulze whispered, awed, too, by this moment of truth and tragedy: "Better give him it, sir . . . We ain't got much more time. The Red barnshitters'll be coming again in half a mo."

Von Dodenburg nodded, but said nothing.

From the Russian positions they could hear the drunken cries, the "urrahs" and the *politruks* yelling, "*slava krasnaya armya*" – "long live the Red Army."

"*Fuck the Red Army*," Schulze said routinely. Like all the old hares, he understood Russian. Some said these veterans of years on the Russian front spoke better Russian than their native tongue.

Von Dodenburg nodded. He took out his pistol and clicked off the safety catch. He didn't dare look at the dying boy. But the boy on the pavement watched him intently as if it were important – very important – to record every move his CO made.

Suddenly, startlingly, the mortar barrage stopped. But the echo went on and on, resounding in that stone waste of death and destruction.

Von Dodenburg raised his pistol. He took aim. Tears were streaming down his worn face now. It took all his strength and willpower for him not to break down completely.

On the pavement, the dying boy began to smile. It was a look of almost pleasure – anticipation, as if he was glad that it was happening to him at last.

Von Dodenburg's knuckle whitened on the trigger as he took first pressure. The boy's face filled the whole of his sight, neatly dissected by the central bar. He forced himself to control his breathing. Von Dodenburg knew that if he missed now, he'd never be able to make a second attempt. Now the boy's bloodless lips, fringed with blue, were moving rapidly. He was saying his last prayer. Suddenly von Dodenburg felt sick with rage: rage at the war, rage at himself that he was being forced to do this; even rage at the boy, that he was so seriously wounded that he couldn't be moved and had to end in this terrible manner, shot by his own comrades.

Up front, Corporal Matz was now beginning to snap off tight bursts with his "Hitler Saw" to left and right. A Red Army man – a bearded giant – staggered, a sudden dark red stain spreading across the front of his brawny chest. His paws straggled the air. He looked as if he were trying to clamber up the rungs of an invisible ladder, to no avail. Suddenly he plunged forward, face frowning, as if he couldn't comprehend what was happening to him. He was dead before he slammed down on to the cobbles.

Behind Matz, Schulze, standing bolt upright, ignoring the slugs slicing the air all around him lethally, had opened fire too. He was firing from the hip. He weaved from side to side, spraying the area to his immediate front. Russians fell on all sides. "Try that frigging on for frigging collar size!" the SS giant yelled exuberantly, carried away by the crazy enthusiasm of battle, where nothing mattered but death and mayhem. "*Boshe moi! Los, ihr Hunde* . . . Do you Russian dogs want to live for ever?" He pressed the trigger once more. The machine pistol at his right hip erupted yet again into a frenzied burst of fire.

Von Dodenburg knew they couldn't hold out any longer. They had to make a break for it while there was still a little time left. Still he hesitated, as the dying boy's lips moved in prayer.

Abruptly, the latter's eyelids opened once more. He had finished the Act of Contrition.

"*Jetzt*," he whispered weakly. "Now, sir . . . I . . . I don't mind . . . Lots of luck." The words dried on his cracked parched lips.

Hardly aware of what he was doing, von Dodenburg took that final pressure. The pistol exploded. It sprang upwards, nearly catching him by surprise. But at that range he couldn't miss. The back of the dying boy's head exploded. Von Dodenburg staggered back. The front of his uniform was splattered with great blobs of blood and bone. The boy's skull had shattered. Through the red gore he could see the broken bone splinters, glistening like polished ivory. The kid was dead. That was one wounded SS man who wouldn't fall into the hands of the Ivan torturers.

Next moment and the man he had killed was forgotten. Now it was von Dodenburg's imperative duty to rescue what was left of his survivors.

He shrilled three blasts on his whistle, not daring to look down. It was the signal to retreat. Up front, Corporal Matz rose from his post. He backed off, firing the heavy machine gun from the hip, supporting it the best he could with his wooden leg. He moved past Schulze, still standing upright, firing to left and right, as if this was some pre-wartime exercise on the SS firing range at Bad Toelz.

"Move it, you Bavarian slime-shitter!" he snarled at his old comrade.

"Hamburg hairy asshole!" Matz gasped and pushed on.

Now the men, rising from their holes like grey ghosts from their graves, followed suit, firing and moving back at a half-crouch, giving and taking casualties all the time.

The Russian attackers grew bolder. They knew they were winning after a battle that had taken all night and had cost them half a battalion of Red Guards in casualties. Even the *politruks*, the political commissars and the secret police officers of the NKVD in their green hats, ventured out, urging the attackers in, making a great show of waving their pistols bravely, but being careful not to move too far towards the front.

Von Dodenburg, waiting for Schulze to begin pulling out, grinned crazily. The blood from his head wound trickled down the side of his vulpine unshaven face unnoticed. A Russian popped his head out of a drainage gulley. Under other circumstances the shaven-headed Ivan, a huge grin all over his yellow Mongolian face for some reason, would have seemed comic. Not now however. For he held a stick grenade in his right hand, poised to throw it after the retreating defenders. Von Dodenburg didn't give him a chance to do so. Without appearing to aim, he snapped off a burst. The 9mm slugs slammed into the Mongolian's face, which disappeared into a mass of red gore. He slithered back into the hole, leaving a crimson trail behind him.

Von Dodenburg and Sergeant-Major Schulze were moving back in unison, the one covering the other. They might well have been two desperadoes in a final shootout in some Hollywood Western. But there was one difference: the bullets fired on this April morning of 1945 in surrounded Berlin *killed*!

Ten minutes later the survivors of SS Assault Regiment Wotan had reached the temporary safety of the second line of defence in the *Ku-damm* area: a collection of kids from the Hitler Youth and old men from the "People's Storm", who looked as if they would have done more good sitting around the stove back home, dozing or puffing stolidly at their pipes, rather than wasting ammunition here in the centre of the battle for Berlin. But that didn't worry the SS at that moment. They were glad of the respite. So they guzzled the water greedily from the burst water main or ate the cold "old man"* from the tins they had looted from their own dead, wondering, if they thought at all, how long they had before the ruthless slaughter commenced once more.

All around them Berlin burned and died. The end was close.

---

* Name given to the standard canned SS meat ration, supposedly made from the bodies of old men – hence the nickname – culled from Berlin's workhouses.

Two

It was an amazing sight. Crawling among the shattered buildings, ignoring the Russian shells which exploded regularly on both sides of the once broad avenue, sirens going at full blast, the armoured convoy, decked out in huge swastika flags, advanced on the pathetic bunch of men and youths and worn-out SS veterans defending the last barricade.

"Holy cow!" Matz cried through a mouth stuffed full of bread and meat. "Do my eyes betray me?" He farted with the shock.

"The tip of my boot'll frigging well surprise you!" Schulze answered, "if you let another frigging fart rip like that. Hell and high water, Matzi, the frigging war's bad enough, but them green-gas farts of yours—"

"Hold yer water," von Dodenburg interrupted sharply, as the leading Puma armoured car swivelled its turret cannon and levelled it at the defenders. Now he could hear the buzz of the armoured car's radio quite plainly as the radio operator contacted someone further down the long column of armoured vehicles. "I think, comrades, we're in the presence of brass."

Schulze reacted immediately. He raised his massive right haunch and without the slightest of efforts let loose one of his well-known musical farts, celebrated throughout the whole of the Waffen SS NCO Corps.

"Be my guest, general. Have a ride on that one," he declared emphatically.

Almost as if on cue, the turret hatch of the middle armoured car was raised and the top half of a real general – an SS one to

10

boot, in full fig – made its appearance. It was followed an instant later by an adjutant in an elegant black uniform heavy with lanyards and gold braid. The adjutant, apparently very angry, cried over the general's skinny shoulder, "Report . . . Someone report . . . Has everyone forgotten military discipline here? I say again: *REPORT*!"

Von Dodenburg took his time. Deliberately he put down the sandwich he had been eating, apparently looking for a clean place to do so. On the turret of the Puma, the adjutant fumed, while the SS General looked down at the motley bunch of defenders, as if he had detected a smelly piece of ordure glued to his top lip.

Finally von Dodenburg walked over, apparently casually, to where the two of them were waiting, the motor of the Puma ticking away like a metallic heart, whilst all around the gunners of the general's escort tensed behind their weapons, as if they half expected a massive Russian attack to commence the very next moment.

For over a month now, he had worn the uniform of a common SS man without any badges of rank or decorations. Why should he? His men knew who he was and obeyed him as he was. Besides, their loyalty was to each other, not to the Führer, the Reich, even the "holy cause", as the Party propagandists still called the National Socialist disaster. His and his men's loyalty was strictly to Wotan. The Regiment had become their cause, their homeland, all that mattered. So now he stood looking up at the two officers, the only sign that he was different from the rest of the scruffy, unshaven defenders being the battered Knight's Cross of the Iron Cross dangling from his neck.

"You," the Adjutant snapped finally, after giving him a long, icy stare which was supposed, von Dodenburg told himself cynically, to intimidate him, "haven't you the sense to come to attention and tell me where your damned officer is? And," he added bitterly, "if he's anything like you, he's probably filling his pants with shit at this very moment."

Von Dodenburg took the criticism in his stride.

"Hardly likely, *Captain*," he said with icy emphasis. "Because he's standing here in front of you."

"What?"

"You heard, *Captain* . . . unless you've been eating big beans," he added, using the common soldiers' expression.

The adjutant's face went brick red with rage. He puffed himself up, looking as if he might explode and burst open at any moment, stuttering for words. Finally he opened his mouth, but the SS General, sallow-faced and shifty-eyed, his chest bare of any decorations save the usual ones awarded to "rear echelon swine", beat him to it. "Your rank and status?" he demanded, his voice low and contained, revealing little.

"*Obersturmbannführer* von Dodenburg, *Oberführer*, commander of SS Assault Regiment Wotan – what's left of it." He waved his dirty paw with its collection of battle-bruised nails at the handful of survivors who were staring at the little scene, as if they were viewing something from another world: a happening that had absolutely nothing to do with them.

The General looked interested. "Ah, the celebrated von Dodenburg. . . . I wouldn't have recognised you from your pictures." He raised his voice, "Let me introduce myself, von Dodenburg." He gave the other man a cold smile, but his dark eyes didn't light up. "I am Mohnke, commander of the Führer Bunker Complex and its defence."

Von Dodenburg touched his battered cap with its long tarnished skull-and-crossbones insignia in a perfunctory manner. He wasn't impressed. He had heard of Mohnke. Early in the war he had appeared in front of a secret SS Court of Honour, charged with the murder of fifty Tommy POWs who had surrendered in France. He had gotten away with it and had spent the war in base jobs until he had been brought to Berlin to command the Bunker's defences. He must have thought it a great honour. After all, he would see the Führer every day! Von Dodenburg gave a little smile. Now Mohnke must have realised that he had landed right in the ordure up to the end of his shitting long nose. There was no way out of the besieged city. If the Führer didn't leave Berlin, he would die with him here in the shattered German capital.

"You are amused at something, *Obersturm?*"

Von Dodenburg didn't answer. Why should he? The Mohnkes of the dying "Thousand Year Reich" no longer played any role in his life and those of his Wotan survivors. He remained silent and waited.

Mohnke was obviously in a hurry. Instead of "making a sow" out of this tall insubordinate colonel, he got down to business immediately. At his side, the elegant adjutant fumed impotently. Watching, Schulze gave Matz what he thought was a gentle nudge in the ribs – it nearly knocked the little man over – and in a stage whisper said, "Feast yer glassy orbits on that prick of an adjutant. He's gonna piss down his right leg at any moment. God in Heaven, don't he just hate our Old Man!"

Matz nodded his agreement, licking his lips as he did so, for Schulze, with that red bulbous hooter of his had, as usual, sniffed out a flatman of schnapps. He hoped the big arse-with-ears wouldn't sup it all without giving him a taste of the fire-water.

"*Obersturm*, I have express orders from the Bunker to relieve you of your duties here forthwith," Mohnke snapped. Up the road, the Russians had brought up their damned "Stalin Organs". Now the fearsome multiple-rocket batteries were beginning to go into action, filling the air with their terrible cacophony. Red flame spurted into the air, followed by black fingers of thick smoke. Moments later the missiles came slamming down into the smoking ruins, making them tremble like stage settings. Mohnke swallowed fearfully. "You are to come with me," he ordered. Below, as if to some unspoken command, the driver of the armoured car began to rev his engine; it was as if he couldn't get away soon enough.

"At whose command, *Oberführer?*" von Dodenburg queried.

Mohnke hesitated, as if he were reluctant to impart the information. Finally he realised from the look on von Dodenburg's haggard face that there was no use playing games with one of the SS's most decorated soldiers. He said, "By that of *Reichsleiter* Martin Bormann, the Führer's secretary."

Even von Dodenburg was impressed. After Hitler, Bormann was the most powerful man in the dying Reich. Mohnke saw that his explanation had had an impact. He added hurriedly, "We must leave immediately for the Führer Bunker."

Von Dodenburg recovered at once.

"There is no question of that," he said bluntly.

Next to the General, the Adjutant finally found his tongue. He snorted, "How dare you talk to General Mohnke like that, *Obersturm*! Have you no sense of military etiquette?" His fat jowls wobbled with rage. "You might be a hero, but if you go on like this, I can tell you, you could end up a *dead* one. Mark my words, von Dodenburg."

The survivors of Wotan reacted immediately. They forgot their weariness, the looted food and drink. They were alert and dangerous at once. As if to some unspoken command, they drew back the bolts of their rifles and clicked off the safety catches of the machine pistols. The threat was unmistakeable. There was tension and impending menace in the very air.

Without turning, von Dodenburg raised his voice over the racket being made by the "Stalin Organs" and commanded, "Stand fast, Wotan . . . *Oberscharführer* Schulze, get a grip on the men, *please*."

Muttering something about liking to "get a grip on the fat neck of that Adjutant", Schulze raised a fist like a small steam shovel and threateningly said, "You heard the Old Man. Now stop farting around."

That tremendous raised fist did it. The men stopped "farting around". To their front, von Dodenburg waited until the shattering noise of the last salvo had died away before saying, in a calm voice, "*Oberführer*, I can only obey your order if I can take my men with me, too. I can't abandon them. It's as simple as that."

Mohnke appeared to hesitate. But a new salvo from the Russian rocket launchers hurried his decision.

"All right, *Obersturm*. You can take your command with you, if it pleases you," he relented.

"It does, sir."

But the General with the dark unsmiling eyes wasn't really listening; he spoke sharply and swiftly to the angry adjutant. The man tugged on his steel helmet and, clambering out of the armoured car, doubled heavily to the rear of the armoured column to where the halftracks packed with young SS men waited, their motors ticking, ready to move off instantly. "*Raus . . . raus . . . absteigen!*" he yelled above the slow rat-tat of an ancient Soviet machine gun which sounded like an irate woodpecker. Reluctantly the young men began to drop from their vehicles.

"More cannon fodder," Schulze commented and drained the rest of his flatman, his Adam's apple racing up and down his throat like an express lift. At his side an anxious Matz watched greedily, licking his cracked parched lips. To no avail. Schulze drained the bottle and flung it away into the rubble, with the comment, "Rank hath its privileges, old house . . . Nothing left for you, I'm afraid."

"In three devils' name, you horned ox, you could have saved a couple of sups for yer old comrade."

"These days old comrades don't exist for Mrs Schulze's handsome only son," Schulze answered unfeelingly. "It's every shitehawk out for hissen. Still," he said cheerfully, "there'll be plenty more of that stuff at the Führer's HQ."

"But the Führer don't drink," Matz objected.

"The Führer don't drink! Matzi, if you believe that, you'll frigging believe anything. Old Hitler knocks back the sauce by the bucketful – all those bigshots do. Now, don't keep on standing there like a fart in a trance. Let's get the lads on board those halftracks before the frigging Ivans turn nasty agen."

Von Dodenburg watched as the reluctant heroes of General Mohnke's armoured column took over the positions of the now excited Wotan men, glad to be relieved, at least temporarily, from the sudden death and danger of the front line. In the lead halftrack Schulze raised his machine pistol and fired a wild burst into the sky, yelling exuberantly as he did so, his broad ruddy face wreathed in smiles. It was the signal that all the Wotan troopers were safely on board.

"*Unerhört!*" the Adjutant snapped. "A senior sergeant – and absolutely no knowledge whatsover of fire discipline."

"Exactly," von Dodenburg agreed easily, not put out one bit by the pompous captain's outburst, "all that birdbrain knows is how to kill Ivans . . . Terrible type." He ignored the Adjutant. "Well, General, what now?"

"The Bunker, as I have just said. But we must hurry. There is no time to be lost. The last of the Melmer shipment should have arrived by now."

"The Melmer shipment?" von Dodenburg began, but before he could pose his question, the frightened driver down below in the Puma had slammed home first gear and the heavy armoured car was beginning to move off with the Russian slugs pattering off its armoured hide like heavy tropical raindrops on some tin-roofed shanty. Behind them the Russians came swarming forward. The new cannon fodder would be dead within the hour.

Three

The telephonist had raised her skirt, a petulant look on her face. She was being faced by a difficult decision. As the upper bunker shook yet again under the impact of the Soviet shells landing a couple of hundred metres away, she stared at the run in her last pair of silk stockings. She knew she could stop the run, which would be hidden anyway when she lowered her skirt, with nail varnish. But the bottle of varnish – "Scarlet Seduction" – was her last bottle as well, brought from Paris by one of Mohnke's SS, long missing or dead this April. What should she do? Keep her nails painted and forget the hidden ladder? Or should she forego painting her nails and stop the ladder running any further? After all, the Führer didn't like his female personnel to paint themselves. What was the motto he was always quoting? "A German woman neither smokes nor uses make-up". Mind you, she told herself, as she considered this major problem (for her), his own mistress Eva Braun piled on the war paint. Nor did she lack French frillies and stockings. Why, she changed her clothes at least three times daily, even here in this ghastly bunker. It didn't matter that the underground fortification was full of drunks and sex-mad men and women – even as she had just come on shift, she'd passed a drunken blonde squatting spread-legged in the dentist's chair, waiting to take on a whole line of drunken staff officers who had managed to escape the Führer's puritanical scrutiny for a little while. Still, she had to make a decision – soon.

"Hold it there, girl," a harsh voice snapped, and instinctively, without turning round, she knew the decision was being

17

made for her. It was the "King of the Teleprinters", as the girls of the Exchange called him behind his back. The man was sex-mad. He couldn't get enough of it. All the girls had been forced to submit to his brutal crude drive since they had come into the bunker and he had been cut off from his various posh-painted mistresses.

At the steel door, *Reichsleiter* Martin Bormann, fat, pugnacious, looking like a middle-weight boxer who had run to seed, licked his thick lips as he took in the sight: a slim twenty-year-old girl, but with a heavy bosom, skirt hitched up high to reveal a shapely section of plump thigh with a hint of frilly black silk knickers (very definitely non-regulation) beyond.

"Dammit," he told himself in his provincial Mecklenburg accent, "she is worth a sin or two."

The telephonist waited. She knew what was coming. She'd heard it all before from the other girls. Some had been shocked and bordering on hysteria. Others, in this sixth year of total war, had been hard and even cracked cynically, "In three devils' name, girl, don't carry on so! You'll hardly notice he's got it in yer. Shake yer arse a couple of times and he's so randy it'll all be over . . . in zero comma nothing seconds." And they had laughed coarsely.

Bormann kicked the steel door closed behind him. He checked the little room. Nobody. He was safe. Not that it mattered. With the Führer on his way out now, he was lord and master here. With a bit of luck, when the Führer had finally cleared off for good, he might well be running the Reich under Allied command. He knew how to listen to "His Master's Voice" and then do exactly as he wished. He made up his mind.

"Take 'em off," he commanded. "No, just in case, slip 'em down about yer ankles . . . *Your knickers*," he added, as if she might not have understood. "And stay where you are. *Los Mädchen, ich hab' nicht viel Zeit.*"

She hesitated for a mere second. Then she bent, gripped the elastic of the black silk panties with both thumbs and pulled down yet another "*souvenir de Paris*" from some soldier she'd already forgotten.

Bormann licked suddenly dry lips. He felt his heart beat more rapidly. There was that familiar thickening of his loins. The sight thrilled him: that broad white arse and the sheer silk stockings, held up by frilly black-lace garters. What had the old Mecklenburg farmers said? "All that meat and no potatoes." Those were the kind of hips a man could get his paws on and gain some purchase, the better to ram himself right into that source of all pleasure. "Just hold on to that chair," he ordered thickly, hardly recognising his own voice, face suddenly glazed with a warm sweat. He grabbed for the flies of his bulky, leather-seated breeches.

The girl steadied herself. Should she wiggle her bottom as the others had suggested? Would that make it any quicker?

Eyeing her naked bottom with that dark hairy gap in its centre, Bormann felt himself grow erect. It pleased him. "Forty-five," he whispered to himself proudly, "and as sharp as a howitzer still." She'd better look out. He was going to give her a right good birding.

Deliberately he strode towards her, his erection swinging in front of him like a cop's truncheon. He grasped those plump hips of hers. The hold gave him a great satisfying feeling. "Just hold tight," he ordered, "I'm going to give it to you – *now*! Are you ready?" he grunted, his face almost crimson now with pent-up sexual desire and energy. "You're gonna like this . . . I promise you."

"Thank you, Herr *Reichsleiter*," she answered dutifully.

"*Jetzt gehts los*. Here we go!"

But it wasn't to be.

Suddenly the door behind him flew open. An excited lieutenant of the *Waffen* SS in a mud-splattered uniform stood there, chest heaving, smoking machine pistol held in his bandaged right hand.

"*Reichsleiter . . . Reichsleiter . . .* Melmer's through the Red lines, sir—" The words died on his lips. His excited young face took on an almost comic look, as his gaze took in the scene before him. The woman bending expectantly at the chair, black knickers around her ankles, holding on for support as if

19

her very life depended upon it, and the fat *Reichsleiter*, once prepared for action, now with his penis hanging limply outside his baggy-assed breeches, his face heavy with disappointment. "Caught with his frigging breeches down," a little voice at the back of his brain rasped maliciously.

Aloud, the surprised young officer stuttered, "I'm sorry, *Reichsleiter* . . . I didn't realise that you were . . . ah . . . *busy*. I just wanted you to know, sir, that the last part of the shipment is through . . . *Haupsturm* Melmer begs to report that—"

"*RAUS!*" Bormann bellowed, enraged. "*RAUS . . . RAUS!*"

The young SS officer flew back out of the doorway as if punched by some gigantic fist, leaving Bormann standing there in mid-stride. His glistening angry eyes flew from that tempting naked bottom to the limp flaccid piece of flesh and gristle dangling impotently beneath his pot belly. He touched it with his fist, decided against any handy tricks to revive his flagging lust and was just preparing to fasten his flies once more when the girl turned and asked brightly, "Do you want me to lend a hand, *Reichsleiter*?"

Schulze watched morosely as the convoy carrying the survivors of SS *Wotan* drove into position in and among the ruins surrounding the bunkers of Hitler and his staff. "Perhaps they're going to concentrate on growing mushrooms," he said to himself.

Matz, crouched next to him on the crowded deck of the Puma armoured car, muttered grumpily, "I could tell 'em what they can do."

"Knock it off, Corporal Matz," von Dodenburg snapped urgently. There were SS men crouched everywhere in the ruins. All of them were heavily armed. Most of them were drunk and he could tell by their armrings that they came from every part of Europe. They were renegades, adventurers, high-spirited young fools, who had abandoned their own countries to fight for the failed cause of the "New Europe". Now there was nothing left for them. They'd die one way or another, either at the hands of the Russian enemy or their own people. Such men were highly dangerous. Even the veterans of SS Wotan had to be careful, damned careful, with such men. "This little lot'd slit yer skinny throat as soon as look at yer. Keep your opinions to yourself – *here*." He tapped his finger against his temple.

Matz looked as if he might grumble, but Schulze silenced any attempt to do so with a swift, "The CO's right. Even Mrs Schulze's handsome son's gonna keep his cakehole shut hereabouts."

A few minutes later and the armoured vehicles had been hidden and camouflaged among the ruins, while what was left of the German defenders' artillery fired a few salvoes of precious shells at the Russians to make them keep their heads down during this dangerous manoeuvre, until the crews were ready to make a run for it to the shelters surrounding the bunker.

Von Dodenburg was here, there and everywhere now. The pompous Adjutant had ordered that Wotan's rank-and-file should take shelter among the ruins, where they were hiding the vehicles. Von Dodenburg pounced upon him immediately.

"My troopers go where I go," he snapped angrily. "When I come out of the Bunker again, I don't want to find the poor shits dead or sent off on some shitting Ascension Day Commando." By this he meant a one-way mission from which there'd be no return. "They stay with me. Clear?"

Angrily, the Adjutant lowered his fat face and said nothing. By now the Colonel, together with the two veterans, Schulze and Matz, were hurriedly shepherding the troopers into the outer bunker, dimly lit and reeking of acrid burnt explosive, schnapps and raw sex. Matz, sniffing the fetid air of the long corridor, as if he were scenting some delectable odour, exclaimed, "God in Heaven, it's given me a blue-veined diamond-cutter just to smell the stuff." He grabbed the front of his begrimed, stained breeches to make his meaning quite clear.

"You and a blue-veiner," Schulze scoffed. "You couldn't

find a mattress to exercise the two-backed beast on even if yer had two hundred mark notes sticking out of yer legs –" The words died on his lips as a fat woman came staggering down the corridor, completely naked save for a paratrooper's helmet and boots. She was waving around a bottle of schnapps and blowing wet kisses at the new arrivals.

"We're dead," Matz exclaimed incredulously. "We're frigging dead and have landed in frigging paradise. Holy strawsack, Schulze, this *is* worth frigging dying for. It's a frigging angel!"

But Matz was in for a disappointment. A huge hand appeared from nowhere, seized the drunken female auxiliary and dragged her into a dark recess in the tunnel's wall. But the almost immediate wet, slapping sounds and whimpers of joy made it all too clear what was happening to the "frigging angel".

They passed on. There were drunks, copulating couples, desperate men sobbing broken-heartedly on all sides in that chaotic bunker entrance. Von Dodenburg's face was hard and stony, revealing nothing. Inside, his mind was racing electrically. The Third Reich had broken down completely and irrevocably. These were the men who had controlled all their destinies for six years of total war. Now they were helpless, totally confused and with not a clue as to what to do next. There and then Kuno von Dodenburg made a decision. He and his men were going to get out of the Führer Bunker, indeed out of Berlin, as soon as possible. They were not going to die here. The rats who had decided all their destinies for so long deserved to snuff it. They had lived high on the hog while Wotan and scores of other front-line regiments, *Wehrmacht* as well as SS, had suffered and bled time and time again on the battlefield to keep these rear echelon swine in their French champagne, fine food and fancy whores. Now, as their guide paused and pulled his uniform straight before he stepped into the main bunker, von Dodenburg told himself, "We're gonna run for it at the first possible opportunity." Unknown to the harshly handsome young SS colonel, however, that particular overwhelming decision had already been made for him . . .

"*Hauptsturmbannführer Melmer, meldet sich zur Stelle, Reichsleiter*," the burly young officer with the slicked, black hair bellowed, standing to attention. "Last shipment delivered as ordered, sir!"

Bormann waved his white, pudgy, office worker's hand to indicate that Melmer should relax. He indicated the silver cigarette box on his desk. "Have a cigarette or cigar if you wish, Captain," he said, weighing up Melmer. Now that the Führer was about finished, Bormann didn't care whether or not Hitler knew that he smoked and drank, and also indulged in the forbidden red meat. Hitler and Himmler were such cranks, believing that smoking and eating meat were bad for you. Where they got such crackpot ideas, he didn't know or care. All he knew was that he was going to get out of this madhouse and live to fight yet another day, whatever the Allies thought to the contrary.

Melmer lit a cigarette with a hand that trembled badly. Bormann let him puff the first soothing stream of smoke before saying, "What does this last shipment look like, Melmer?"

Behind him, *Standartenführer* Hackmann, pudgy, bespectacled and unhealthy looking, leaned forward urgently. This is why he had stayed in the bunker in the first place. He wanted to hear what the value of the last Melmer shipment was.

"Four or five boxes are stuff taken from the camps – teeth, rings, glasses, things like that, sir. Useless now that we can't get Degussa" – here he referred to the Reich's chief smelting plant – "to reduce them to bullion bars, sir."

Bormann nodded his understanding and said, "The rest, Melmer?"

"Good, sir. Varied carat weight and sizes, but essentially bar gold, which can be sent elsewhere to be treated." Melmer frowned. Over the years he had come to know a lot about this dirty business. Now, when everything was falling apart and

23

the enemy would start looking for him, the less he knew the better.

Bormann flashed him a warning look and he stopped immediately.

"Thank you," the *Reichsleiter* said, then he asked, "How many crates?"

"Twenty of gold and gold coins plus about two and a half of precious stones, rare stamps and the like, *Reichsleiter*.

The bunker started to quiver once more. Again the Russians were ranging in on the former chancellory area. It was clear that they didn't know exactly where the bunker system was located. But they'd find out soon enough. All the same, the Ivans were getting dangerously close, and Melmer wanted to be off and away while there was still a chance of getting out of Berlin.

Bormann made him wait. By nature the fat Party boss was a selfish sadist; he was concerned solely with his own affairs. People were just numbers to him, to be used and forgotten. He looked thoughtful. Behind him, *Standartenführer* Hackmann cleared his throat like the jumped-up clerk that he had once been. He put his pudgy fist in front of his dingy rotten teeth, as if he wished to hide them so that they would cause no offence to his "betters". He said, "I wonder if—"

"You shitting wonder too much, Hackmann," Bormann rounded upon his subordinate. "Piss or get off the pot."

Hackmann was not offended. The Hackmanns of the Third Reich were never offended; they felt they couldn't afford to be. Even if his boss had thrown that celebrated pisspot in his fat face he would still have been his usual crawling polite self. Hackmann, in short, was a born third-rate politician. "I was thinking of the final destination of the – er – shipment, *Reichsleiter*?" he completed his query, as humble and as polite as ever. Inside he tensed, waiting for the fat pig's answer. It was going to be vital, if he were to carry out his own bold mission, the thought of which made him feel giddy even now. Where had he suddenly acquired such breadth of vision? Such boldness? All the same, coming down to earth again, he told himself, without the Melmer gold, his great plan was doomed from the very start.

Bormann considered for a brief moment. He, too, had plans. In fact, they were already being put into operation. Still, the fewer people who knew about his future intentions for Martin Bormann the better. He turned to Melmer for a second. "Thank you once more, *Hauptsturm*. I'll see the Führer is informed of your bravery and devotion to duty. There'll be the German Cross in Gold in it for you."

Melmer faked enthusiasm. "Thank you very much, sir," he chortled. At the back of his mind a harsh cynical voice snorted, "Bormann can stick his German Cross in Gold right up his fat arse – *sideways!*" He raised his right arm in salute. "*Heil Hitler.*"

"*Heil Hitler,*" Bormann replied routinely and without enthusiasm. "On your way out send that SS hero von Dodenburg – or whatever his name is – in." Bormann waited until Melmer departed to become a footnote in the history of one of the most terrible episodes in World War Two. "Destination, you ask, Hackmann?"

"Yessir." Hackmann tried to conceal his eagerness, keeping his gaze fixed on the dusty concrete floor to hide the look in his eyes.

Bormann paused. "There is only one place, isn't there?" he exclaimed rhetorically, lying as he uttered the words.

"Is there, sir?" Hackmann was genuinely surprised.

"Yes, we shall fight on. There is no doubt about that. We wait only for the Führer to make his decision and then the last battle, *which we shall win*, will commence."

Hackmann's heart sank. "Naturally, sir . . . And where?"

"The final destination for the Melmer Gold? Why Hackmann, you idiot – *the Führer's Eagle's Nest . . .*"

Four

Now things were moving fast. Despite the drunken chaos of the Bunker, supplies and vehicles were arriving for SS Assault Regiment Wotan with surprising speed. There were two new Renault tanks, driven by volunteers of the French SS Division *Charlemagne*; Skoda self-propelled guns, also new, as if they had just been produced in Occupied Czechoslovakia; great four-wheel drive Wehrmacht trucks straight from the Ford factory outside Berlin, manned by Russian *Hiwis**. Indeed, it seemed to a sweating, harassed von Dodenburg that half of Europe was conspiring with the leaders of the dying Third Reich to ensure they'd be able to spirit away their treasures. As Schulze, helmet stuck carelessly at the back of his cropped head, gaspingly pointed out: "Great Crap on the Christmas, even the shitting Americans are on our side now!" He indicated the freshly painted trucks now arriving from the General Motors factory.

Von Dodenburg smiled cynically and accepted a slug of French cognac (*Standartenführer* Hackmann, in charge of the supply operation, was being very generous). As he had commented while his servants handed out captured English cigarettes, beer and French cognac to the SS troopers, "Nothing is too good for our brave boys, von Dodenburg." And he had rubbed his palms together like some provincial shopkeeper happy that the money was rolling in.

"For the time being, you big rogue," von Dodenburg answered Schulze. "Wait till the crunch comes. Once Big Business

* Russian volunteers from the German POW camps for captured Red Army men.

26

has taken its loot and made a run for it, no one will want to know the nasty Nazis and their dreadful crimes."

"Tick-tock in the pisspot and clap in yer cock, sir, eh?" Matz had grunted.

"Something like that," the CO had agreed, and then he was off again to check the loading of the precious crates that the fat *Reichsleiter* so concerned about.

Schulze watched him go, tall, lean, but with his shoulders bent a little, as if with care.

"The Old Man shouldn't worry so much about us," he said, taking another hefty slug of the Martell cognac.

"*Alte Schule*," Matz said, eyeing one of the drunken female auxiliaries who was bent double, retching and heaving up stale beer from the night before. "Old school, that's our Old Man. First the lads and then himself – a long way behind . . . Talking of behinds," he raised his voice, "look at that officer's mattress and what she's showing *behind*."

"Holy mackerel!" Schulze exclaimed, as he followed the direction of Matz's gaze and was confronted by a naked bottom, fringed with jet-black pubic hair. "I could eat that with a gold spoon."

"But you're not going to," a pedantic, irritated voice broke in.

The two old hares turned as one.

A fat, bespectacled SS officer with the badges of a general on the lapels of his black uniform stood there staring down at them severely. "You've got work to do, you know. Time waits for no one – and remember, our beloved Führer is in residence. He has his eagle eye on everyone and everything." With that he waddled away, with Matz grunting, *sotto voce*, "And you'll have the toe of my eagle-eyed boot up yer fat arse if you don't watch it, too."

Still, the two of them had been in the SS far too long; they realised it could be dangerous, especially now when they were shooting even SS officers out of hand for the slightest dereliction of duty, to be found lazing about at the Führer's bunker. They decided to get up and pretend to work.

"Let's go through the motions, Matzi," Schulze said wearily.

"Yer," his old running mate agreed. "Blind 'em with bullshit. I'll see if I can find a bucket and pretend I'm doing something."

"That's the way," Schulze said, "corporals carrying buckets. Fools 'em every time. I'll accompany you. Pretend I'm giving yer orders or something. Now find yer bucket, old house."

Matz made an unkind and perhaps impossible suggestion as to what Sergeant-Major Schulze might do with his bucket. But the latter took it all in his stride, remarking in a good humour that he would be unable to carry out Matz's proposal "on account of the fact that I've got a double-decker bus up there already, old friend."

Thus engaged, wandering around with a holed bucket, Schulze rapping out orders whenever he spotted anyone he thought important, the two old hares came across the old man talking to the black-clad boys of the Hitler Youth. Indeed he was doing more than just talking. With a hand that was shaking badly, as if he had an acute case of the DTs, he was clapping the undersized boys on the cheek fondly like a favoured uncle; or even seemingly tickling them under their chins, as if attempting to bring a smile to their pale, strange, childish faces.

"*Nanu*," Schulze exclaimed, pausing in mid-stride, as he watched the old man, bent and clad in a shabby, too large military coat, cuddle yet another youth warmly. "What have we got here? What's that dirty old fart up to, Matzi?"

"No good, in my opinion," his comrade said, lowering his holed bucket, as if it was an almost unbearable weight. "Rotten old pervert – and him in uniform too. What next?"

"By the looks of that coat he must be in the Party. By the looks of him, too," Schulze added, "he's *warm*." The big NCO meant homosexual.

"Lot o' trash in the Party these days," Matz commented, watching as the dirty old man seized the hand with which he had just patted the Hitler Youth in short pants with his other one. It was as if he were trying to stop the left hand from running away independently, it was trembling so badly. "Not like in the good old days." Matz puffed out his chest proudly, as if he had been a leading member of the National Socialist Workers' Party and not one of the Bavarian Folk Party, which had earned him the nickname of "the Bavarian barnshitter" in SS Assault Regiment Wotan. "The Führer wouldn't have tolerated that kind of piggery."

"*Einverstanden*, Matzi. What do you think? Should we report the dirty old fornicator—"

"For God's sake," von Dodenburg's voice cut into the conversation. "Don't you know who that is?" he hissed, not knowing whether he should laugh or cry at Matz's last remark.

"Who?" they asked in unison.

"*The Führer!*"

"Holy strawsack," Schulze exclaimed, "I thought he was one of them nasty, dirty old men, who give sweeties to innocent babes-in-arms. But the Führer's a big feller, who shouts all the time. That old fart looks as if he'd drop dead if he raised his voice."

Von Dodenburg was tempted to agree, but at that very moment, Adolf Hitler turned, and with a bemused smile on his ashen face, he started to toddle back to one of the entrances to the underground bunker complex, trembling all over. Von Dodenburg came to the position of attention for a moment, but then relaxed almost immediately. The Führer hadn't even seen them. He was, apparently, too concerned with finding his way back into that concrete tomb. Then he was gone and, farting gently, as if in accordance with the solemn mood of that moment, Schulze said softly, "We shall not see his like again, sir, I fear."

Matz looked up askance at his comrade. Schulze winked just as solemnly and von Dodenburg, still shaken a little at what, as Schulze had correctly predicted, was probably his last glimpse of Adolf Hitler, said, "All right, sort 'em out, Schulze. Then stand them down for an hour – and see they get some good hot fodder inside them. The men are going to need some decent food for what is soon to come."

Sergeant-Major Schulze was tempted to ask the CO what exactly that mission was. But he desisted. The "Old Man" looked worn out as it was; why burden him any more? "What about hitting the hay yourself, sir, for an hour or two till it's dark? I can take care of things, can't I, Matzi?"

Matz snorted and made no comment.

Von Dodenburg forced a weary smile. At that moment he felt like he could sleep for a week solid. But he knew that was not to be. He had to get his men out while there was time still. His recent glimpse of what was obviously a dying Hitler had reinforced him in that view. "Thanks, you big rogue, Schulze . . . I appreciate the thought. But we're having our last planning conference at" – he cast a hasty glance at the cracked dial of his gold watch, once presented to him by the Führer himself in those glory days when he had won his Knight's Cross of the Iron Cross – "seventeen hundred hours. So I'd better be off." With that he was gone again, striding energetically to his appointment, as if he were the old Kuno of the good days instead of the near mental wreck of April 1945.

Schulze again watched him go. He shook his head, but didn't comment on the "Old Man". Instead he turned to Matz and said, "All right, let's get on the stick, old house. Rustle up some good fodder for the boys. They can all have some suds," by which he meant beer, "but not too much. A sniff of the barmaid's apron and those Christmas Tree soldiers'll be keeling over right, left and centre."

"More for us," Matz said gleefully.

But Schulze's usual good mood had vanished. He looked at the darkening sky, broken here and there by the myriad fires that raged in a circle around the trapped last defenders of Berlin, and sighed.

It was an unusual sound for him and Matz chirped, "Got yer monthlies agen, Schulze? Feeling blue?"

"You'll be frigging feeling *black and blue* in a sec," the other man retorted. But there was no anger in his voice, just a sense of resignation. "Come on, let's sling our hook, comrade."

They slung their hooks.

Hackmann watched them go. His brain was alert and very busy. For that pudgy bureaucratic appearance of his belied a quick alert mind, always ready to seize the main chance. He had come a long way from being a provincial teacher in a one-horse Eifel village where he had taught classes of rural, thick-witted louts up to the age of thirteen, when they had been finally joyously released to the freedom of their tiny fields. Now it was vital that he didn't let this last chance slip. For Heiner Hackmann sought glory. He wanted to go down in the history books and it was at this moment of absolutely over-whelming crisis, when the leadership had lost its head and chaos reigned, that he could achieve that aim – that is, if he kept his head, too.

He knew Bormann's plans. He'd stay in Germany in the hope that he'd be able to negotiate a future for himself with the new Allied bosses. If that failed, Bormann obviously thought that the Melmer shipment, soon to leave the Bunker, would see him through his declining years in great luxury. Bormann's solution was the one he expected from his long-term boss. It was that of an arsecrawler who was playing both ends of the field, hoping he'd come out of the stinking mess smelling of roses.

Hackmann had other plans for himself. But in order to carry them out, he needed that gold, the Melmer loot Bormann was now about to send southwards to the Eagle's Nest, forwarding the SS convoy through that narrow strip of land between the Russian and Western Allied fronts that still remained in German hands.

Hackmann suddenly licked his bright red, thick, sensualist lips, as if they were abruptly very dry. The Führer had always boasted that he had started to reform the old corrupt Germany with exactly seven followers, ordinary Bavarian working men – and look what he had achieved within the space of a decade? At the beginning of the National Socialist revolution, the Führer had possessed virtually nothing – no money, no backers, no power base – just his own determination. He, Hackman, had much, much more to build upon and commence a new German revolution after the defeat soon to come. But he *did* need money – lots of it. The South Americans might play at being fascists, but they were a weak, corrupt folk. They'd pay lip-service to the new party starting in their midst, safe from Allied interference, but it would be hard *Ami* dollars that would open the door and make the new party base secure, until the time came when the new National Socialism could return to its German homeland and claim what rightfully belonged to it.

He smiled thinly at his own thoughts as he turned and proceeded with ever increasing speed back to the bunkers, for the Russians had commenced yet another barrage. Bormann thought he was in control. He had prepared the escape route southwards to the Eagle's Nest with the utmost care, as was his wont as Party Secretary, with the various regional *Gauleiters* at his beck and call. But what Bormann had forgotten was that it had been he, Hackmann, who had done all the spadework, made all the arrangements and finalised the escape route.

Now, everywhere, he had cronies, agents, spies, paid underlings who would take orders from him as if they came from Party Secretary Bormann personally. Bormann might think he was in charge. In reality he, Hackmann, was. The last Melmer shipment would go where he wanted it to go. As the first Russian shell slammed down a hundred metres or so away, its blast sending him flying into the dank fetid passage of the side bunker. Hackmann was filled with a sudden joy, the like of which he had never experienced before.

Five

There was no doubt about it. This was the start of the Russians' final attack. The low sporadic bombardment which had commenced two hours before had merged with the obscene stonk of the mortars, the snap-and-crackle of small arms fire, the high-pitched hysterical hiss of the machine guns, into one massive overwhelming barrage, which seemed to go on forever.

Hidden in their cellars, crouched low in the pitch darkness – they had extinguished even their guttering candles in order not to attract prowling Russian rapists – the surviving civilians of Berlin could hear the rusty rumble of tank tracks and the stolid steel-shod step of the advancing infantry. Everywhere the Russian armies were gathering up their strength for that final assault. They packed every ruined street, bomb-cleared space, dank debris-littered alleyway.

Those who still had any strength or courage left packed their single escape suitcases, rucksacks, even plain sacks, which would be tied to their backs when they emerged from their cellars and made their desperate run for it. Old people were propped and tied into invalid chairs, prams, even the four-wheeled *bollerwagen* in which they had once hauled firewood and potatoes. Those who couldn't be moved were made drunk, given poison, sleeping pills, for they were to be abandoned to their fates. That said, even the grannies among the females were painted with red spots so that they appeared to have some disease such as syphilis and would be killed cleanly, rather than being gang-raped and *then* murdered by the Ivans.

Others were already burying their treasures. Determined to stay and stick it out – after all, the sad popular song of that spring proclaimed, "*Es geht alles voruber . . . es geht alles vorbei*,"* and the Ivans couldn't be that bad – they hid their pathetic bits and pieces. They might well help them – that valuable Bavarian stamp, the odd piece of Dresden china, the miniature by Menzel – to start a new life once the initial horror of the Russian takeover had passed. Those who were leaving mocked them: "Don't bother . . . Take yer hindlegs in yer paws, old friend, and make a run for it, while you've still a chance. With what we did to the Russkis in that frigging Soviet paradise o' theirs, you can't expect one bit of mercy. The Ivans are going to eat us Germans alive, for frigging breakfast!"

And all the while the guns continued to thunder, that terrible overture to the lethal opera soon to commence.

Meanwhile, just as trapped as the rest of his collapsing nation, and while Bormann watched, leaning against the sweating concrete wall of the bunker, chewing as usual, for he seemed to eat all the time now, Hackmann briefed them yet again. Von Dodenburg didn't like the burly Party boss, nor his pudgy assistant. All the same he listened carefully. They had the latest information about the state of the front. As Bormann had exclaimed, "My Party officials have stayed in office, not just the fine *gauleiters* and *kreisleiters*, but the ordinary little people: clerks, parish telephonists, post office counter attendants. The *Amis* need them too, you know. Those little people keep me constantly informed, better than those monocle Fritzes" – he meant the Army generals – "who are virtually all traitors or are ready to surrender at any minute. After all, they're crapping their pants, most of them," he had ended his explanation contemptuously.

Von Dodenburg had nodded his agreement silently. For once Bormann had been telling the truth. As always it was the little people, ordinary honest humble folk, who did more for their country than the bemedalleed heroes and fat corrupt Party bosses.

* "Everything passes".

34

"The plan is," Hackmann was explaining, "to turn right into the path of the Ivan attack, not the main one, but one of their flank assaults. They'll never expect anyone attempting to escape from the Bunker to do that. Besides, we'll be posing as Russians, won't we?"

Von Dodenburg assented sagely, "Of course, we have the Russian *Hiwis* driving most of their armoured vehicles. Those renegades will do their utmost to get the SS safely through the Ivan lines. Their own lives depend upon it. The Russians will shoot the Hiwis out of hand, without so much as the offer of the 'condemned man's last cigarette'."

"Once out of Berlin," Hackmann continued, "we shall turn south west and, keeping the River Elbe on our right flank, proceed south. There the territory is still firmly under control, though we do know that the *Amis* are heading into Saxony, bound obviously for Leipzig."

"Yes, so much is clear," Bormann said as he swallowed the end of the salami sausage he had been eating. For a supposed vegetarian like the Führer, he had developed a sudden great appetite for meat, von Dodenburg told himself cynically. "The situation becomes a little more clouded and uncertain as far as Franconia and Upper Bavaria are concerned. That cowboy general of the *Amis*, Patton, seems to have penetrated deep enough to have surrounded Wurzburg. But that is still a long way off Munich, and it goes without saying that the holy of holies, the Mountain at Berchtesgaden will *never* be taken!"

Hackmann sniffed. It was a small gesture, but von Dodenburg, his nerves on edge as it was, noticed it immediately. Abruptly he realised with the total clarity of a sudden vision that there was rift between master and servant. Hackmann was preparing to go his own way, whatever Bormann, his boss, thought to the contrary. Once out of the Bunker, he told himself, Bormann's orders would be forgotten immediately.

The pudgy bucreaucrat looked at Bormann and then nodded to von Dodenburg.

"Perhaps, *Obersturmbannführer*, you'll give us the military side of the breakout now?"

Von Dodenburg didn't hesitate. He had been doing these briefings now since September 1939. Sometimes he seemed to be doing them in his sleep. He stepped forward and tapped the map nailed on the wall by means of two bayonets.

"We head straight for Berlin-Wedding, already in Russian hands. Up front we have one of the frog tanks, the Renault. It looks a bit like an Ivan T-34 tank. The crew will be mixed *Hiwi*-SS. With a bit of luck we'll fool the Russians and be through before they can tumble to the fact that we're not what we're supposed to be. Their communications, as all of us front swine know, are piss poor. It'll take them an age to alert their rearline units that we're not what we're supposed to be. By then we should be in open country and on our way southwards, general direction Crailsheim." He tapped the southern city on the map.

"And the Melmer shipment?" Bormann asked urgently.

Before von Dodenburg had a chance to explain the convoy's make-up any further, Hackmann jumped in urgently, "I am personally taking care of the Melmer business, *Reichsleiter*. We shall be in the middle of the convoy, with armour to our front as the *Obersturm* has just explained, and armour and SS infantry in halftracks to the rear. I feel that that is the best defensive position, *Reichsleiter*."

"Excellent," Bormann snapped, pulling out another length of salami from the pocket of his baggy riding breeches and taking a hearty bite of it.

Lounging against the wall, Schulze whispered out of the side of his mouth to Matz, "Turd eats turd."

"What do you expect, old friend, from a shit like Bormann?"

Bormann frowned as if he might have caught the comment. Von Dodenburg certainly had and he went on hastily, in case Bormann started asking awkward questions.

"The essence of a successful breakout, gentlemen, is this: surprise and speed. Once you've caught your opponent off guard, you've got to move fast and keep up the momentum till you're out of danger. It must therefore be clear to all ranks that we haul arse . . . or, as the immortal Sergeant-Major Schulze would put it, '*marschieren oder krepieren* . . . MARCH OR CROAK'."

It was quite dark now. The Russian barrage had died down somewhat. Here and there, however, white tracer zipped through the night sky with electric lethal suddenness. Cherry-red fires, still burning from the afternoon, flickered and twisted in an eerie circle around the trapped men in the bunker area. Despite the occasional explosions and sudden sharp bursts of fire when jumpy sentries fired at some shadow or figment of their own imagination, there was an eerie brooding silence about the bunker and its environs. It was as if something – something *terrible* – might start at a moment's notice. Indeed, von Dodenburg, clad in an earth-coloured Red Army blouse with a Russian forage cap on the back of his cropped blond head, walked as if on eggshells, taking care not to raise too much noise.

Schulze and Matz, for their part, were indulging themselves in the shadows with a couple of the "*blitzmädchen*", female signals operators, from the communications centre. They were very young, but drunk and willing, as if nothing mattered any more. Indeed, they didn't even insist that the two old hares used contraceptives to avoid pregnancies. As Gerda, the taller of the two said, slurring her words, "Why do we need frigging Parisians" – by which she meant contraceptives – "we're not gonna live long enough to find out whether we're pregnant or not. Now stick it to me, Sergeant Schulze, hard and deep so that my glassy orbits pop."

"Anything to oblige a lady," Schulze said and did just that, while a metre or so away, Matz's girl moaned in ectasy, "If you'd have only tied me up in the dentist's chair, Matzi, you could have done anything you liked with me, you filthy swine."

"Christ Almighty," Matz moaned, the sweat pouring down his crimson face with the effort, "what do yer think I'm doing—" He never completed his sentence, for a little sexual complication brought it to a rather abrupt end and for a while at least, he wasn't interested in the perverted tastes of nubile teenagers who desired to be tied down in dentist chairs.

Up front in the lead French tank, chatting to the *Hiwi* commander in broken German and Russia, von Dodenburg checked the minutes off by the green-glowing hand of his wristwatch. The timing had to be exactly right, he told himself. He knew the Russians of old. The Red Army was not as efficient as the German one, but it was just as bureaucratic. Their assaults always ran to the same pattern: a barrage, a harangue by the *politruk*, the glass of vodka, the patriotic song and then the assault formation would come marching out (sometimes even with a brass band) in mass formation, shoulder to shoulder, crying "*Urrah*" and perhaps realising that most of the front rank would be slaughtered, but that there were others behind them to take their places. The Red Army, it seemed, had an inexhaustible supply of manpower.

Now, von Dodenburg hoped, the Russians would attack in the centre – the signs of a mass attack were all there – leaving the escape column to ease its way round the left flank and into the Berlin working-class suburb of Wedding. He prayed he was right. For they were all out in the open now. It took only a single enemy flare and they would be exposed, trapped in the enemy's merciless fire.

Suddenly, startlingly, the brass band some two hundred metres away struck up one of those swift noisy Soviet marches. The blare of trumpets and the bass beat of the big drum echoed and re-echoed down the ruined streets. The Russians were about to attack. Already von Dodenburg could hear the first hoarse drunken cries of "Long Live the Red Army . . . *Slava Krasnaya Armya!*" Flares started to shoot into the night sky and explode with a soft plop, illuminating all below in their garish red and green hues.

"*Davoi?*" the sergeant enquired from von Dodenburg, both their faces hollowed out to glowing deathheads in the eerie unnatural light.

"*Davoi!*"

The sergeant kicked the shoulder of the driver below in his compartment. He pressed the starter. There was a throaty whirring. It grew louder by the instant. Abruptly the engine sprang into life. The Mongolian driver hit the gas pedal. The roar of the engine rose to a crescendo. Suddenly the night air was filled with the cloying stench of petrol. All along the line the drivers started up. The darkness was shattered by the racket.

Now gunners tumbled behind their weapons in the turrets and cabs of the halftracks. There were cries, orders, curses in Russian and German. Up in the lead tank, von Dodenburg waved the illuminated signal disk, once, twice, three times. Below, the Mongol in the driver's seat rammed home the first of his dozen or so gears. The Renault jerked. Its tracks clattered, as if in protest. They caught. With a lurch that threw the two men backwards so that they had to grab for a stanchion hurriedly, the light tank moved forward.

Von Dodenburg flashed a look behind him. The column was following. He searched for the customary vehicle that wouldn't start. But this night they were all beginning to move. No one, it seemed, wanted to be left behind to the tender mercies of the Ivans.

For a moment he remembered all the times that SS Assault Regiment Wotan had moved out at dawn or dusk, driving into the unknown and the bloody merciless battle that would undoubtedly come sooner or later. Six years of it, winter and summer, year after year. He saw once again the Vulture with that monstrous beak of a nose of his, Brothel Creeper, One-Egg and all the other thousand upon thousand of young men – a sheer unending column of silent wandering ghosts – who had gone this way, never to return. He shook his head firmly to dismiss those spectres. This was no time for the past, he told himself. It was the future that counted now. So many had *died* for Germany. The time had now come to *save* what was left for that same Homeland. He pressed his throat mike and commanded, "*Tempo . . . tempo!*"

Just next to him in the open turret of the Renault, the

Russian *Hiwi* sergeant grinned in the lurid light of the flares falling from the skies like doomed angels, and growled back, *"Tempo*, Mr Boss!"

Further down the column, Sergeant-Major Schulze, in no way excited or happy at the prospect of the escape attempt, growled to Matz, his old running mate, "Buy combs, lads . . . there's lousy times ahead."

Matz said nothing. It was better not to do so. The column rolled on. A few minutes later it had disappeared into the glowing darkness.

Six

Piotr yawned. He scratched himself. He was lousy again. The lice were stirring in the warmth under the blanket. All of them were lousy and they'd remain so until the Fritzes were finally finished here in Berlin and they came to the end of the long road from Stalingrad.

Next to him, the German woman whimpered. He patted her, his lust satiated for a while. She had come to him the night before and showed him her naked breasts – skinny little things with pathetic pink nipples, not like the massive ones of Russian women, ideal for suckling children and comforting men. Then she had raised her skirts and showed him that she was naked beneath. Her body too was skinny, even pathetic. There were no "love handles" for a man to grab hold of, and her pubic hair was sparse and pale like that of a child.

"*Sauber* – clean," she had whispered fearfully.

His German wasn't very good, but he understood what the Fritz woman wanted. She was placing herself under his protection so that she would not undergo the mass rapes that the other women hidden in the cellars were suffering. He had nodded and ordered "*Davoi* . . . du schlafen nun," and he had indicated the rough bed of filthy, lice-ridden blankets. She had obeyed immediately.

Obediently she had spread her skinny legs and revealed the pale pink of her sex. That had been enough for him. He had needed no other stimulant. He had grown hard immediately. But she had been boring. No fire in her. Rape was better, more exciting, but he knew she was safe. He wouldn't get pox from her. He had taken her gently, sparing her. For she seemed as if

41

she might break if he took her roughly. Indeed, he had prodded her a mere six times during the night. Nothing.

Now he woke slowly, like a man does after a good night of vodka and sex, with no pressing problems before him. At this stage of the war he was no longer risking his neck for the Fatherland. Old Pock-Face – he meant the Soviet dictator Stalin – would have to win the rest of the war without him. Besides, here in the east of the beleagured city, the fighting had died down. The main Russian attack was due to go in this morning, right into the centre, and crush the Fritz defences around the bunkers for good.

He yawned again and shrugged and wriggled mightily, as the lice reacted to the movement.

"Bastards," he cursed softly. "*Boshe moi* – why did the Almighty ever create lice? What use were they?"

Next to him the Fritz girl gave a soft moan and stirred yet again. He felt himself slowly begin to harden. He held up his brawny left arm to the emerging dawn light and gazed at the half-a-dozen German watches he'd looted which were strapped there. Nearly six. The men would be starting to make their tea and morning porridge soon. They'd had their rations of *kishka*, small dried fish, the night before; now they've have to do with the porridge. Besides, somewhere around they'd be able to loot food if they were hungry enough. His erection grew even harder. Yes, if he was going to do it, he'd better get on with it now. Soon he'd have to get up and carry out the usual dawn inspection of their perimeter. Boring but necessary. That damned political commissar, Dewniak, the Ukrainian bastard, was just waiting for him to slip up so that he could have him arrested.

He slipped his big brawny hand between the sleeping girl's skinny thighs. He felt the heat. His erection hardened even more at that warmth. Gently he touched her. She was wet. She stirred more vigorously. He pushed her on to her back. She didn't object. But she kept her eyes tightly closed, as if she didn't want to see what was going to to happen to her.

"Never fear, little bird," he said, "Papa will be gentle with his little Fritz." He threw up the front tail of his shirt, ignoring the lice now in his overwhelming lust, and with a grunt, thrust it into her. Her spine arched and her stomach rose to meet him. He grinned. "You don't mind the old piece of Russian salami after all, do you Fritz Fräulein?" Then the time for talking was done and he concentrated on his pleasure, breathing hard as he plunged that hard roll of flesh in and out of her skinny loins.

"Grosse Kacke auf'm Christbaum," Matz hissed. "Someone's dancing a frigging mattress polka in there, Schulzi!"

"I didn't think they were baking a frigging cake to welcome us, you stupid streak o' piss." He moved forward, the "Hamburg Equaliser", his father's brass knuckles, dating back to the old man's days on the docks, gleaming on his massive right fist. "Come on," he instructed.

Matz followed, heading for the sound of hectic panting. Behind them the line of SS panzer grenadiers, armed only with clubs, bayonets and grenades (as a last resort) pressed themselves even closer to the shadows and waited, hardly daring to breathe. For the Ivans were all around them and it was growing lighter by the instant.

Schulze looked at the entrance to the cellar. He realised, old hare that he was, that this was the Ivan CP. A few hastily scrawled signs in Cyrillic script, a flag and the sole radio mast in the whole area indicated that this was the Russian Command Post, for only senior commanders had the use of radios in the Red Army. He nodded significantly at the radio mast. Matz replied in the same silent manner that he understood.

Together they entered the ruined stairwell. The panting urgent sound was growing louder. Matz grinned and thought of the surprise to come. The Ivan was not going to like that particular form of surprise, but still, the little Corporal told himself, he shouldn't go around screwing foreign women at this time of the morning. Totally unnatural, at least for Russkis.

Carefully, very carefully, they crept forward. Through an

open door they could see a group of Russian soldiers sprawled out on the floor of the room, sunk in a heavy drunken sleep among the vomit and empty bottles of looted schnapps. Behind them the first of the troopers entered. Schulze indicated the Russians with his right hand. "Deal with the sleeping beauties," he mouthed the order. The man nodded.

They mounted the stairs. They were close. They could hear the woman's moans quite clearly now – and she was enjoying her seventh rape of that night.

"*Tiefer, du dreckssau!*" she was hissing fervently between her moans. "Deeper . . . deeper, you dirty sow!"

Matz licked his dry lips and wished he could change places: "It ain't frigging fair, our women spoiling them hairy-assed Russkis—"

"*Schnauze* . . . shut it!" Schulze cut him off hurriedly.

They turned and there they were, lying on the floor in a mess of blankets beneath the CP radio, writhing and heaving totally naked now as they reached their climax, the skinny girl's legs clasped tightly around the Russian's neck, her face contorted and glazed with sweat in this final moment of passion.

Matz made a hitting gesture, but Schulze shook his head firmly. "Let 'em have a last bit o'fun, for God's sake, Matzi."

Suddenly the woman screamed. Her white body arched, as if she had been stung. Piotr gave one last mighty thrust. Then both of them, sobbing as if they had just run a great race, collapsed on the blankets. Next moment, Schulze hit the Russian a mighty blow on the point of his bearded chin with the "Hamburg Equaliser". There was a sharp click. The Russian's head shot back, his neck broken. He was dead almost before he realised what had hit him.

The woman screamed again, as the dead Russian slumped across her. His weight pinned her down. She was going into hysterics as she tried to push him away, her face contorted crazily. Matz darted forward. Schulze had no time for that. Let her have hysterics. Still, he wanted her silence. Before Matz could stop the woman screaming, he lashed out, not as hard as before, but hard enough. The woman reeled back.

Already her cheek was beginning to colour a livid, blood red. Schulze didn't wait for the cheek to swell. "Forget the gash," he urged. "Get the radio – quick, for chrissake!"

Matz smashed the butt of his machine pistol into the old-fashioned military transmitter. It shattered. But already the damage had been done. The screams had aroused the Russians below. There were cries of rage, bewilderment.

"*Stoi?*" someone challenged angrily. "*Boshe moi . . . stoi?*"

"Holy shit!" Schulze cried. "Now the clock is really in the pisspot!"

Next to him, Matz reacted immediately. He swung round. He didn't seem to aim. The machine pistol chattered at his hip. Suddenly the room was filled with the acrid stench of burnt cordite. Shell cases tumbled to the floor in a brass-shining cascade. The Russians pelting up the stairs were animated in a crazy dance of death. At that range, Matz couldn't miss. They went down on all sides. Arms and legs flailing, they seemed to waste away in front of the two comrades' wide, gaping eyes.

Schulze pulled the hysterical girl free from the weight of her dead rapist. "Not much in the upper storey," he told himself automatically, as she revealed her tiny naked breasts. "Couldn't get me head between those and keep my eyes warm on a cold night."

Brrr! The vicious burst of fire ripped along the length of wall behind him. Plaster rained down. A clump of metal slammed into his shoulder and he staggered. The girl screamed and Matz yelled over the sudden crackle of small arms fire coming from below, "You hit?"

"Of course I'm frigging hit!" his comrade snorted and, ripping off with his machine pistol, sprayed the stairwell with a rapid burst. Screams, shouts, curses. There was the sound of men falling heavily.

"Fuck this for a tale of soldiers!" Matz cried.

"You can say that again," Schulze yelled back, ducking as the fire from below was renewed. "The frigging Reds have gone and got us with our hooters right in the horse manure. *Fuck*!"

"We're trapped?" the girl gasped, wrapping herself in a blanket, oblivious already to her dead lover, now staring with sightless eyes at the bombhole in the ceiling.

"Well, I don't think they're going to invite us to a frigging tea-dance with frigging fancy cakes," Schulze answered with heavy humour. Then he forgot the girl. "Matz, we've done what we should have, we've alerted the shitting Ivans."

Matz nodded gloomily, "You can say that again, *altes Haus*. Now what, eh?"

It was the same question that *Obersturmbannführer* von Dodenburg was asking himself some two hundred metres away, as he crouched next to Hackmann near the line of stalled vehicles.

Hackmann, as scared as he obviously was, knew the answer to their problem instantly: "The Ivans are occupied. They're busy with your patrol. We can use that to slip around their flank and be on our way before they fetch up reinforcements, *Obersturm*," he suggested rapidly.

Kuno looked at him incredulously, as the red and green signal flares started to shoot up over the Russian positions, indicating that the Ivans were calling urgently for reinforcements. "You can't mean that?"

"Mean what?"

"That I should abandon my men just like that." He snapped his fingers angrily.

"Yes. What are a few lives in comparison with those of the many . . . not to speak of the goods," he added somewhat mysteriously, "which we carry and which can have an important influence on the future?"

On any occasion, von Dodenburg would have dearly loved to have heard more about this strange "Melmer shipment" that Bormann and Hackmann had talked about. Not now, however. The fate of Schulze, Matz and the rest of his brave young troopers of the reconnaissance patrol was much more important. "Damn you, Hackmann," he snapped.

"You can't talk to me, a superior officer, like that—"

Hackmann began angrily. But Kuno was no longer listening. He pressed his throat mike and switched to net.

"To all," he commanded urgently, "make smoke . . . Make smoke . . . Mortar crews, too . . . We're going in." He changed back to his own vehicle, confident that his own men and even the *Hiwis* would act without discussion. If nothing else, they knew their own lives were forfeit, if they didn't remove the barricade up front immediately. It wouldn't take the Ivans long to bring up reinforcements. Then they'd be trapped in a real ding-dong battle from which there'd be little chance of escape.

"Driver . . . driver advance," he instructed, then turned to the *Hiwi* sergeant, next to the two SS officers in turret. "All right, Stefan . . . Give 'em stick," he ordered above the sudden roar of the tank engine as the Renault surged forward.

The Russian grinned, displaying a mouthful of stainless steel teeth. "Stick it is, *Obersturm*," he yelled back. "Those Ivans'll soon fill their pants when they see it's us from the SS."

Von Dodenburg smiled at that. The attack commenced.

47

Seven

"Why do your men always curse, use that filthy depraved language of theirs?" Hackmann asked testily, as they squatted among the exhausted troopers in the cover of the apple orchard. Here and there the aidmen were still busy tending the wounds of those who had been hit in that mad charge to rescue Schulze's squad and press on eastwards. "It's always 'frig' and 'shit' and 'piss' and the like. Don't they know any other words, eh?" His eyes glinted angrily behind the pince-nez he affected in imitation of *Reichsführer SS* Heinrich Himmler, his supreme commander. "Tell me that, pray, *Obersturm*."

Kuno dabbed a scratch on his left cheek with a dirty handkerchief. That "pray" made him want to puke. What a pedantic pisspot Hackmann was. In civilian life he could well have been a schoolmaster; he looked the type. "I agree. Once, though, they did know fancy words, like 'Good morning' . . . 'I think it's going to be a nice day' and all that kind of *shit*," he stressed the word maliciously. "But that was long ago, before they became front swine."

"What's that got to do with it?"

"Front swine live, eat, *crap*," again he emphasised the crude word, "and sometimes die in holes in the ground, called slit trenches. They make handy pre-dug graves by the way." He grinned at Hackmann and the latter flushed. "So what can you expect from men brutalised in that manner? Life is too hard, too short for fancy words. We've left all those famous polite euphemisms behind for the civilians and rear echelon stallions, who have time to play the gentlemen."

Hackmann's flush deepened. "I think you are playing games with me."

"Think what you like," Von Dodenburg snapped back. He stopped dabbing his face and his hand dropped to his pistol holster significantly.

Hackmann recognised the significance of the gesture, but he persisted. "Remember my rank. I expect and deserve the politeness which is duly accorded it."

Von Dodenburg opened his mouth to spit out a bitter retort and comment on what Hackmann might do with his exalted SS rank (honorary). But the radio operator of the command halftrack beat him to it. He rose from the back, crouched, with the earphones still attached to his head.

"*Obersturm*," he yelled urgently. "A blitz for you, sir . . . From the Führer Headquarters." His voice indicated that he was impressed, as hardbitten as he was, to receive a signal from such an exalted place.

"Who's it from?" Hackmann asked urgently, his concern with the swearing habits of the front swine forgotten now in his eagerness to know what lay in the signal.

"Bormann," von Dodenburg snapped, as he watched the signaller's hands move expertly across the keyboard of the enigma machine, while he followed the groupings on paper.

"What does he say? Hurry! . . . please hurry, *Obersturm*," Hackmann said.

Von Dodenburg cut back the hot retort. After all, he was curious too. Why was Bormann signalling them at this stage of the game? What was so important?

Minutes later he knew why and, squatting under the apple trees once more, heavy with white spring blossom now, he read the message out aloud, while to their front the "air sentry" surveyed the blue sky with his binoculars for the first sign of enemy fighters which had been buzzing the area ever since first light. Obviously the Ivans were on the lookout for escapees from Berlin like themselves.

"Please report your positions every twenty-four hours from now onwards. STOP. Reports coming in of deep American penetrations of our lines in Saxony STOP. Imperative reach Berchtesgaden soonest. STOP. Await new orders on the spot. END."

The two of them stared at the decode in silence, disturbed only by the muted drumroll of gunfire in the distance: the continued Soviet barrage in Berlin. Finally, von Dodenburg broke the silence with, "Well, what do you make of that last sentence, Hackmann?" He had already dispensed with giving the Party hack his SS rank.

Hackmann didn't seem to notice the implied insult; he was too busy trying to decipher the meaning of those last words too: "Await new orders on the spot". Who was going to give those orders? It couldn't be Himmler. He was in the north of Germany trying to save his precious hide working out a peace deal with the Western Allies. Nor Goering. He was in the area. But Bormann had already thrust him out of the Party and sent the local Munich SS to arrest the fat air marshal in his Austrian castle.

"The Führer – is he going to head for Berchtesgaden?" von Dodenburg cut in, his ears already aware of the faint hum of aircraft engines in the distance, the sound boding no good for the survivors of SS Assault Regiment Wotan.

Hackmann considered and then shook his head. "I don't think so. In his infinite wisdom, it seems as if the Führer is detemined to stay in the Berlin bunker and fight the Bolshevik enemy to the bitter end. No . . . No," he stuttered, for the sudden thought had upset him. "I think it's *Reichsleiter* Bormann himself."

Von Dodenburg shot the other man a sharp look. "But why should he signal us that *now*? It's hardly twenty-four hours since we last saw him in the *Führerbunker*. It seems very strange to me."

Hackmann considered. He could guess why Bormann had decided to flee the Bunker. The Führer had finally made his mind up. He would stay and die in Berlin. Bormann had other ideas. It was Bavaria and Berchtesgaden for him. But before he fled, he wanted to secure the Melmer treasure. Obviously it

50

was vital for his own personal plans too, and Hackmann could guess what he'd do with the Melmer shipment if his other political intentions came to nothing and the Western Allies wouldn't play ball with this German turncoat. But he decided not to tell the arrogant young swine at his side. He would use von Dodenburg as long as he needed him and then he'd get rid of the bastard. Till then it was better that von Dodenburg knew as little as possible. He shrugged. "*Reichsleiter* Bormann has never taken me into his full confidence, *Obersturm*," he said simply.

Von Dodenburg's lean haggard face flushed angrily. "But you must know something. You can't have worked for so long with *Reichsleiter* Bormann and—"

He stopped suddenly. The noise of aircraft was getting louder. There was something menacingly purposeful in the increase of engine noise, as if the pilot had abruptly spotted a target and was about to go to work on it.

"What is it?" Hackmann asked, suddenly alarmed too.

Von Dodenburg didn't answer. Instead he shaded his eyes against the slanting rays of the weak Spring sun. To his immediate right, a formation of three planes were coming in fast and he didn't need his identification tables to recognise them. He had seen the type often enough in the past, on every tank battlefield in Russian.

"*Stormovik dive-bombers!*" he bellowed, hands clapped around his mouth. "Air alarm . . . Soviet dive-bombers!"

Fifty metres away, Schulze threw away his hunk of salami and almost dropped his bottle of looted vodka, though being the dedicated sauce-hound that he was, he didn't. "Holy strawsack," he yelled, as everywhere the *Hiwis* and the SS troopers scattered and raised their weapons, ready to take up the new challenge from the air, "now even God's gonna shit on us!"

The gull-winged bombers started to beat up the terrain between them and the stationary column, coming in at ground level, the propellors whipping up the grass below into a green fury.

Next to Schulze, Matz, equally religious, crossed himself and intoned in a pious but hurried voice, "For what we are about to receive may the good Lord make us truly thankful." Then he ducked as the first salvo of bombs came whistling down with lethal intent . . .

Nearly a thousand miles away, a group of bespectacled men dressed in tweed jackets with leather patches at the elbows and baggy Oxford flannels, lounged in their battered armchairs, much as they had done all their life in the common rooms of Oxford and Cambridge, chatting now in the desultory manner of men who had all the time in the world. Here and there one of them remembered his tea and sipped it before it became stone cold and nibbled one of the rationed biscuits. Outside in the grounds of the pseudo-Gothic Victorian manor, someone was playing a very leisurely game of tennis with a lady dressed in long baggy shorts: the first game of the season. The soldiers with bayoneted rifles slung over their shoulders didn't stop and watch; the lady in question was nearing sixty and held no physical attraction for the sex-starved soldiers serving out their time in this remote closed and highly secret society.

Apart from the soldiers, and the unkempt man busily engaged hopping around the lawn digging up a turf or two and then moving on to repeat the exercise with obsessive energy and determination, it could have been a typical pre-war English scene.

But these middle-aged civilians and the occasional tweed-clad lady, who looked as if she had been a dab hand at wielding a hockey-stick in days gone by, were more important than a whole division of well-armed and trained infantry, perhaps even two such formations. For this was Bletchley, the heart of the British government's secret enemy decoding operations, and the men and women drinking weak sugarless tea fought their own remorseless battle against the Nazi enemy – frontline fighters in that dirty war in the shadows.

But on this particular sunny April 1945 afternoon, the war

on the continent seemed to have gone into its final lull. British operations had ceased practically everywhere save on the River Elbe, where Montgomery was preparing to make his last river assault of the war; and also in the south, where Patton and Patch's American divisions were racing ahead into the Alps with hardly any opposition. Indeed, most of the ex-dons who staffed this remote Home Counties establishment were already considering how long it would take them before they could relinquish their present appointments and return to their various pre-war chairs – Oxford and Cambridge, naturally.

But already the messenger from Hut Three, cycling crazily across the grounds which separated the Nissen huts from the main house, was bringing them the Ultra decode which would spoil this quiet English teatime for the former dons.

The unkempt man, slightly demented obviously (but then most of them were really), stopped his digging for a moment and yelled at the messenger-cyclist, "I still haven't found it . . . Damn nuisance."

"Keep trying, Alan. You're sure to get lucky soon . . . Dig away!" the cyclist replied, waved dangerously and rode on, leaving the place's mastermind to keep on digging for the "treasure", a hundred pound's worth of silver coins of the realm which he had buried back in 1940 when it was thought the Germans might invade. "Treasure," he snorted with every thrust of the spade, "a fortune in treasure . . ."

Finally the cyclist reached the house. He flung the Ministry of Works cycle down, burst into the tearoom and cried, in a distinctly non-Oxbridge accent, "Come on, me lucky lads and lasses. . . . I've got a corker for yer."

Spoons rattled. Tea was spilled into chipped saucers. Someone swallowed one of the rationed biscuits quicker than he had intended to and broke into a fit of old man's coughing. A querulous voice cried angrily, "I say, can't a chap drink a cup of tea in peace and quiet? . . ."

The messenger from Hut Three did not hear. He waved the decode and yelled, "Pin back yer lugs, you Romans, the rats are leaving the sinking ship in Berlin. Bormann's coming out. We've work to do chaps – plenty of it. *The game's afoot, Watson*, as dear old Sherlock would have said, and we need the bloody Bradshaw . . . *To work!*"

Part Two
"C" Takes a Hand

*"There is only one arm of the Armed Forces
in which the British are our superior:
it is their Secret Service."*

Adolf Hitler, 1940

Part Two

Take-a-Hand

One

"*HITLER MISSING . . . RUSSIANS FIGHTING CENTRE-BERLIN. HIMMLER MAKES PEACE OFFER THRU SWEDES . . . WAR NEARLY OVER.*" The London news-vendors were shrieking their latest with an enthusiasm that had been absent from their hoarse boozer's voices for years now.

Lt. Commander Mallory, his head full of the latest infor-mation from Bletchley, had become a cynic over the last six terrible years of war. But now, for the first time in a long while, he believed the headlines. For once the Ministry of Informa-tion was telling the truth. The Huns were still fighting, but once the Russians bumped off the Führer in Berlin or what-ever they were going to do with him when they captured Hitler, which would be soon, the rest of the Third Reich would collapse like a house of cards. Already the parlour pinks and those who had fought the war with their mouths were talking of the socialist utopia and the brave new world of the so-called "Welfare State", which that nice old upper class gent, Mr Beveridge, was proposing.

Mallory pushed by the crowds eager to buy the latest editions and entered White's, nodding to the top-hatted at-tendants and handing in his name. As always, Commander Mallory was astonished at the way this London club seemed to be the meeting place for the top names in British Intelligence and, indeed, served virtually as an office for their discussions of national intelligence secrets. He smiled at the thought. No other country would have tolerated such laxity but then, Britain *was* different from the rest of the world. It was with that thought uppermost in his mind, that the head of "Mallory's Marauders" was ushered into the presence of the exclusive club's most powerful member.

"C", the head of MI6 or the SIS, as it was known to its members, was hunched at the bar, sipping carefully at a double whisky held in his claw of a hand. For a moment or two before "C" deigned to notice him, Mallory studied the head of British Intelligence, one of the Empire's mightiest organisations, even though, officially, MI6 did not even exist.

Surprisingly enough, despite the press of important civilians and high-ranking officers all around him, "C" sat alone, with plenty of space between him and the nearest members. He was a skinny, pale-faced man with thinning grey hair, dressed in a light grey suit. Indeed, everything about him seemed grey, as if he had just emerged from a long stay in a dust-filled closet – or *grave*, a harsh voice at the back of his mind corrected him. The only splash of colour in the Intelligence Head's whole outfit was his Old Etonian tie.

Mallory finished the drink that someone had handed him, probably on the orders of one of the chief's minions, who lurked in the remoter regions of the exclusive club. He tugged at his shabby dark blue tunic, adorned with the ribbons of DSO and DSC and then cleared his throat noisily.

It worked. C turned his skinny neck, as if it were controlled by rusty springs. Their eyes met in the mirror behind the bar. C seemed to have difficulty recognising him. But Mallory knew that was only a pose, meant to put his subordinates in their place. He winked. C frowned. He wasn't used to being winked at. Mallory didn't give a damn: he'd seen through many an inflated reputation in these years of total war. C nodded. He was to approach that august person.

Mallory mumbled a greeting. C did the same. "Drink?" Mallory thought he caught the offer. Before he could reply, a double whisky appeared in front of him. He accepted it gratefully. Scotch was like gold these days; only the Yanks could afford it.

Time passed. Important people came and went. Occasionally one or two of them nodded formally to C. A few smiled. But not many. As for C, his face, as grey as his suit, remained somber and unsmiling. He might as well have been dead, Mallory thought.

"Good of you to come, Commander," C said suddenly. The voice was no longer so fruity and upper-class as Mallory remembered it from the old days – "posh and pound-noteish", as his Marauders would have said.

"It's all right," Mallory heard himself answer. He seemed always to say the same words, as if it were a great honour to be received by C. Which it wasn't: C always meant problems, and all too often, sudden death.

"Best of all places to meet you," C added, as he always did when they met at White's. "Good club, good chaps and a crowd like this is always the best cover. No one would expect you to be here talking about affairs of state, what?"

"Yessir," Mallory answered dutifully, though from his experience the people who came to the exclusive club were always talking openly about affairs of state. Perhaps they thought that the working-class servants who manned the place didn't possess ears or minds.

"Berlin – it didn't work?" C snapped suddenly, completely out of the blue.

Other officers might have complained. It was not on to spring a question of that complexity on a person before giving him a chance to collect his thoughts. But by now Mallory was accustomed to such a haughty, upper-class manner. He said simply, "No, sir. Mission too difficult. Not prepared to risk my chaps' lives. It's outlaw country between our lines on the River Elbe and Berlin. Russians, Germans, DPs" – by which he meant wandering "displaced persons", as they were called officially – "and thousands of odds-and-sods, killing and looting each other. Wouldn't have stood a chance in hell in infiltrating through that mess – even my Marauders, sir."

"Understood," C said, voice revealing nothing. "All to the good, as it turns out. I need you on another mission. Hitler will, we know, die in Berlin. The Hun already belongs to history. It's the others we're concerned about, and their plans – *for the future*, Mallory." He emphasised the words as if they were significant.

"I didn't know the Huns *had* a future, sir. I thought we were going to castrate the men and put their womenfolk in army brothels?" Mallory risked a mild joke.

But irony was wasted on C. "Splendid idea, Mallory. It'd serve the Hun right. But democracy –" He shrugged his skinny shoulders and left the rest of his sentence unsaid, as if the concept of "democracy" explained everything.

"Yes, democracy, sir," Mallory laid it on. "The bloody Greeks have a lot to answer for inventing the whole concept."

"Very true." C dismissed the problem with a weak wave of his clawlike hand. "Have you ever heard of the Melmer Gold, Mallory?" he asked. Old as he was and apparently dying visibly on his feet, C had an amazing degree of flexibility mentally. His mind appeared to be able to jump from topic to topic effortlessly, like that of some smart kid.

"No, sir."

"Right, then I shall explain – and please regard this as the last and greatest secret of the current bit of unpleasantness."

Mallory would have smiled at the old-fashioned usage – "bit of unpleasantness" – but he was too intrigued by what C had to tell him to consider the matter. "I will, sir," he snapped.

"Good. I have your word on it?"

Mallory nodded. Carefully, C took a sip of his drink, as if that cunning devious old mind of his was still considering whether he should tell Mallory what he knew. He looked through half-closed eyes at the commander in his shabby tunic. Even the ribbon of his DSO seemed faded and worn, and what with the black eye-patch where his left eye had been shot away some time or other, the man looked as if he were ready for beaching on half pay – but C knew that Mallory and his handful of military criminals had been worth a brand-new destroyer in the many exploits that they had carried out since D-Day. He put his glass down and took the plunge.

"Melmer was, is, a low-ranking captain in the SS," he

commenced in a low voice, so that Mallory had to lean forward and strain to hear him clearly, "a kind of glorified messenger boy really. Still," C added thoughtfully, "he'll become an important footnote in the history of World War Two if his role ever does become known . . . which I doubt. There are too many interested parties, not only in Germany, but also in the rest of Europe, perhaps even on the other side of the big pond, for all I know." He smiled weakly.

It was a C joke, Mallory told himself. The old man bloody well knew that this mysterious Melmer had something to do with the other side of the Atlantic Ocean.

"It's Melmer's task to bring shipments of precious stones, gold, foreign currency to Berlin – to the Reichsbank to be precise – where it is dealt with."

"Dealt with, sir?"

"Yes. Made clean, with all traces of its origin removed, so that it can be used on the international market with no questions posed as to its origin. Our bankers do love to have clean, unsticky fingers." C actually tittered like a naughty schoolboy enjoying the discomfiture of his elders.

Mallory dismissed his surprise. "Origins, sir?" he snapped sharply.

Not far away at the bar, a fat rear admiral looked round somewhat indignantly and wondered how such a shabby, broken-down humble commander dare make so much noise in White's. Then he spotted C and turned away quickly. It didn't do to get mixed up or on the wrong side of that man; you'd probably find yourself serving in some God-forsaken port in the Far East if you did.

"You've heard of the German camps?"

"Where they put their workshy, communists and the like, sir?"

"In a way." C wasn't giving away more than necessary. "Well, in the occupied territories of the East, the Huns have other camps where they are – were – making considerable amounts of money from, let's see, goods they take from their prisoners and the work they do for the great German industrial complexes. Unfortunately, some of their prisoner-workers die, and they don't want that known, nor the fact that they are the source of such wealth."

Mallory frowned. He was still puzzled. But he didn't stop C. When C talked, most wise people remained silent and listened. It was safer that way. The old man was steeped in tricks and "trade" secrets.

"Now, this wealth, under heavy SS guard naturally, was brought regularly to Berlin – to the Reichsbank to be processed, as I have already said. From there, in its new guise, it was shipped to other European countries for further use—"

"What other European countries?" Mallory couldn't restrain himself. "After all, the Jerries dominated virtually the whole of Europe until D-Day."

C looked at him, as if he were an innocent babe still sucking on its mother's tit. "My dear boy," he exclaimed, "don't be so naive. Switzerland, Sweden, Spain and the rest of the supposed neutral countries all wanted the Hun to win. Sixty per cent of Switzerland's industrial production went to Germany in 1944 – everything from chocolate to anti-aircraft guns. But that amount of imports had to be paid for. The Swiss, those ancient defenders of all that is precious to us in the form of democracy," he laughed maliciously, his little faded eyes almost disappearing in his wrinkles as he did so, "wouldn't accept payment for their goods in worthless Nazi marks. They wanted the oldest and best international currency of them all: *gold*!"

"Melmer's gold?"

"Exactly."

C took another sip of his whisky. His skinny chest heaved as if the effort of so much talking was too much for him. Mallory took the opportunity to slip in a quick question. "There is still a shipment leaving Berlin, sir?" he hazarded a guess.

"Already left, my boy. We've just had a confirmation from those parlour pinks of ours in Bletchley." He frowned. "In other times, we'd have arrested the bunch of them – crypto communists, the lot. No matter." He clicked his thin fingers weakly. "No matter. This particular shipment is particularly worrying to us. We're very concerned about where the Melmer gold is going. It's pretty obvious that Germany is virtually beaten and will be in need of no more Swiss precision arms and that excellent coffee of theirs. So where is the stuff bound for?"

Mallory hazarded a guess. "Perhaps some Nazi big shot wants it for his own use, now the rats are leaving the sinking ship?"

C clicked his tongue testily. "I wish you wouldn't use those Americanisms. These days everyone uses that 'okay' of theirs," he said pronouncing the US word as if it were some disgusting obscenity. "Even the PM does. But then he is half-American after all. Possibly, Mallory, you're right. Save for one thing, the Nazi big shot, as you phrase it, is a certain Martin Bormann – you won't know who he is, but he's the power behind the throne, more important than Hitler himself, and it is he who is behind the shipment, and it looks as if he is to follow it to the south of Germany."

"To what purpose?"

C shrugged his shoulders carelessly, but his faded eyes were anything but careless. "Let me just say this, Mallory. I want you to pick half a dozen of your best chaps – one of whom speaks fluent German."

"I have a former German in my group, sir."

C chuckled; an eerie sound from that skeletal person. "I know. Ex-communist. Better watch him. You never know. Once you've worked for 'Uncle Joe', you *always* work for him. There is no escape from the Reds, save death. Well, as I said, half a dozen of your best chaps and arrange to fly out to Germany immediately. All arrangements have been made. You have top priority."

"Where, sir?" Mallory asked, his pulse quickening at the thought of one final action before the long war ended, and he was faced with years of boring office jobs in the Admiralty, if their lordships deigned to keep on a broken-down old one-eyed salt.

C looked squarely at him. "Frankfurt . . . to see the Supreme Commander, General Eisenhower."

"Ike!"

"Yes, you're going to be briefed personally by General Eisenhower. The mission is that important – and remember, top secret as well. Once it's finished, you must forget it. It will be as if it never happened. No mission and no Melmer shipments, clear?"

"Clear, sir," Mallory stuttered. Hardbitten and cynical as he was, he had been taken completely by surprise at his master's revelations. "But—"

"Remember," C cut him short, "you are not to reveal *anything*, now or later." He lowered his voice to a mere whisper. "And remember, too: don't trust *anyone* – Allied or enemy. This April we are dealing with something that will never be revealed to the world, and there are people out there who will stop at nothing to prevent that great secret being publicised."

"Yessir, I understand," Mallory assured the spymaster, though he didn't really understand at all.

C took out his gold half-hunter from his fob pocket, consulted it and said, as if they had just been engaged in a mild chat about the state of the April weather, "I've enjoyed talking to you, Commander. Now, I mustn't detain you any longer. Give my regards to you know who."

Flustered and definitely puzzled, Mallory accepted the out-stretched hand. It was cold and bloodless, like that of someone ready for an early grave. Minutes later he was outside again in the noisy London street with the barrage balloons sailing overhead like tethered elephants, wondering if the conversation had really taken place.

Two

Patton pushed his way to where his aide, Colonel Codman, was waiting, surrounded by gaping GIs in their battle gear. In the distance outside the little town there was the muted sound of a fire-fight still going on. The US infantry of Patton's Third Army hadn't cleared the area totally yet. But at this moment Patton, the fire-eater, had other matters on his mind than the clearing of Merkers.

"They're here, Charley," he announced. "You checked everything?"

"Yessir. We're all set to go." He hesitated. "But the elevator's a bit primitive, sir."

Patton, tall, immaculate, his helmet with its outsize three golden stars gleaming, waved his riding crop in dismissal. "If the Supreme Commander wants to see for himself, he gets to go. After all Charley, Ike's the boss." He winked. "Who knows, he might make a fool of himself. After all, as you say, the shaft is two thousand feet deep."

Codman gave an inner sigh. Patton was always in the business of upsetting his superiors, as long as he came out of it smelling of roses. " 'Kay, sir, we can go."

"Lead on, McDuff."

Watching from the edge of the crowd of curious GIs, many of them trying to get a photo of the Top Brass with their looted Leicas – there were even a few with autograph books in their hands – Spiv said to Mallory, "What a shower. I've shat better soldiers than that lot. Autograph books indeed!" The little ex-cockney barrow boy spat contemptuously into the dry white dust that came from the great salt mine far below.

Mallory laughed shortly. "They won the war, Spiv. It's going to be the American century, y'know."

"Damn capitalists," Thaelmann, the ex-member of the German communist party, said in that grumpy Teutonic manner of his. "We have saved the world for the monopoly capitalists."

"Something like that," Mallory stated, thereby, ending the discussion as soon as it had commenced. "We're going down in the second cage."

"Is it safe?" Spiv asked.

"You'll soon find out, mate," said Peters, the ex-Guardsman originally from the North East's pit country. "They say it's a quick death, Spiv."

The little cockney raised his middle finger: "Sit on that," he suggested.

His old comrade took it in his stride. "Can't, old mucker. I've got a double-decker bus up there already."

That two thousand foot drop into the heart of the salt mine where the treasure was located had occupied the minds of the Top Brass, too. Eisenhower and his army group commander Bradley looked at each other in a worried manner as the ancient winding engine started to grunt and groan alarmingly as it took the weight of the lift packed with the senior American generals.

Patton, the gadfly of the US military establishment, was in his element. Aloud, he started to count off the numbers of gold stars on the shoulders of the brass. Then he looked up at the single wire cable barely visible in the diminishing patch of sky. "If that clothes-line should part," he observed to no one in particular, "promotions in the United States Army would be considerably stimulated."

Out of the growing darkness Eisenhower growled, "Okay, Georgie, that's enough of that. No more cracks until we're above ground again; 'kay?"

"'Kay Ike," Patton said with a smile and lapsed into a happy silence.

Finally reaching the bottom of the salt mine, with gawping infantrymen everywhere in the dimly lit cavern, wondering obviously why the Top Brass had turned up here without warning, they stumbled their way forward. Behind them, now accompanied by Brigadier Gault, Eisenhower's personal aide, a typically cheerful Guards officer, Mallory and his two men followed.

Their route seemed to last endlessly, as Spiv commented: "Cor fer a duck, get lost in this place and yer'd end up like salted beef."

Gault laughed softly, "Soldier, I wouldn't even think that thought if I were you. The very mention of it gives me claustrophobia."

Spiv didn't know what the word meant, but he guessed it signified something unpleasant. He said, "Me lips is sealed, sir," and shut up promptly.

Mallory told himself it was probably the first time that Spiv hadn't babbled on incessantly ever since he had first met the little cockney crook in one of the Army's correction centres, otherwise known as the "glasshouse."

Finally, stooped low, they passed through a long tunnel to emerge into a high vault, illuminated to a brilliant incandescent white by a battery of hissing US Army issue Coleman lamps.

Gault caught his breath sharply as he saw what the chamber contained. It was piled high with open crates of gold coins and raw gems. Everywhere, propped against the rough white walls there were Old Masters. There were even dusty great albums of postage stamps, embossed with the gold crests of their former noble owners.

The GI guarding the treasure nearly dropped his rifle at being confronted so abruptly by the Top Brass, faces he knew only from the newsreels back home in the States.

"*Jez-us H. Christ!*" he breathed increduously.

Next to Mallory, Brigadier Gault did the same. "Gosh," he breathed too, "a real treasure trove. Look at that – Durer . . . And over there Titian, Van Dyck . . ." His voice trembled with awed shock.

Only Patton wasn't impressed. He threw a bored glance at the artworks and said, "They look to me as if they might be worth a couple of bucks, Ike. Kinda stuff you see behind the bars of bordellos back in the States."

Together with the US Army Signal Corps photographers, who were scheduled to take the Top Brass's photos for the world's press – for after all, this was the greatest treasure ever found by the US Army – came the German guide. He spoke fluent English with an American accent and immediately got to work attempting to impress the illustrious visitors with statistics and facts. "Over there, gentlemen," he babbled, "you can see the entire payroll of the German Army for the month of April."

Bradley, the Army Group Commander laughed, "I doubt the German Army will be meeting payrolls much longer." He turned to Patton. "If these were freebooting days when a soldier kept his loot, you'd be the richest man in the world."

As always Patton was ready with a quip. "Yeah, I'd give every GI in my Third Army a pension for life and what was left over, I'd use to buy the newest weapons to fight our former Russian ally."

Eisenhower frowned. "Georgie," he said severely, "that's enough of that. Walls have ears, you know." He indicated the German guide. "Besides the Russians are *still* our allies, you know."

"Yeah, Ike," Patton said, though there was no remorse in his voice. Indeed he added a moment later, speaking in a whisper, "If you believe that crap, you'd goddam believe anything."

After his photo had been taken whilst staring down at some ornate crowns and similar regalia stolen from some noble family in the German-occupied East, Eisenhower nodded furtively to Gault.

The British Brigadier understood. He dug Mallory in the ribs. "The Supreme Commander wants a quiet word with you. Over there," he indicated a spot near the wall, close to a giant eighteenth-century nude in oils. "Make it sharp. It's one devil of a job getting a solitary moment for poor old Ike. I swear, if they could, they would have a guard sitting next to him when he goes to the thunderbox."

Mallory grinned and did as he was ordered.

Eisenhower was poised next to the fleshy Rubens nude. He was little different from when he had awarded Mallory the US Silver Star for bravery the previous December, though now there were deep dark circles under his eyes and he was wearing discreet make-up to hide his almost prison-like pallor. Still, the old ear-to-ear grin was not lacking when he smiled and commented, "I hope none of those Signal Corps jerks decides to take my photo next to that nude. Mamie—" by which he meant his long-suffering wife back in Washington – "would have my hide, that's for sure." He held out his hand. "Good of you to help us out again."

Mallory took the soft weak grip and stuttered something about being pleased to help. He could see why Ike was such an Allied success. He was as hard as nails beneath that smiling exterior, but all the same he knew how to send people to their deaths happy and grateful to go.

"All right, Commander," Eisenhower said hurriedly, eyeing the tough sailor with his black eye-patch and livid scar running the length of his cheek, where the shell splinter had hit him and taken out his left eye, "I'll make this fast. You may be wondering why I'm meeting you like this?"

Before Mallory had time to agree, Ike went on fast, looking to his left and right to check whether he was being observed, while Brigadier Gault kept guard at some distance to keep away any interference. "I'll tell you. I'm surrounded by people I can't trust – my own people, ones I've known since West Point," he added bitterly. He nodded at Patton, waving his arms in his usual high-spirited fashion. "General Patton is a good soldier, one of the best. But he represents big business. Anything I let slip on such matters and sooner or later the boys on Wall Street get to know about it. Commander, you understand?"

Mallory nodded his understanding. Of course he did. Once

this war was won, then Ike would go into politics just like Grant had done before him after the end of the Civil War. These generals weren't politicians, but they were popular heroes. Any political party in the United States that signed up the ex-General Eisenhower, Victor of the "Crusade in Europe", as Ike himself called the battle for the Old World, would be on a winning ticket.

"So Commander, I'm faced with a very difficult situation, not militarily, but politically. You have been briefed about the Melmer shipments?"

Mallory nodded.

"And you know that the last and perhaps biggest one is heading south from Berlin at this very moment?"

Mallory nodded, but didn't comment. He knew that Ike wouldn't want him to. Every minute was precious and the Supreme Commander would want to get the matter off his chest before anyone else broke in.

"Now I want that shipment nobbled, that's what you British call it, eh?" Eisenhower raised an anxious smile for a fleeting moment. "With no fuss. If it comes out like this business here in the mine, people back in the States are going to ask *too* many questions and the answers they'll get won't please them one bit. They'll find out that not only German industrial giants were involved in the exploitation of slave labour in the East, but *American* ones here in the West. What would the Great US Public make of it when they heard that Ford made trucks for the Krauts, using slave labour?" He looked at Mallory grimly. "And that's only one American firm. What about US firms in South America, which supply Nestlé in Switzerland with coffee beans to make this new *Nescafé* that they've been selling to the Krauts since 1943? We'd open a whole can of worms and you British wouldn't come out of it too good either," he said as an afterthought.

Mallory said nothing, but inside he raged. Was this what the good honest old Tommy Atkins and GI Joe had been fighting and dying for? So that international firms with no conscience could make money, hedging their bets so that whatever side won, *they'd* come out of it with increased profits?"

Eisenhower read the look on Mallory's hard, battered face and said, "Yeah, I know what you're thinking, Mallory. I feel the exact same. But there's nothing we can do about it. Those firms are too big for us. Perhaps one day –" he broke off and shrugged a little helplessly. "But for the time being at least, we've got to keep the lid on this dirty business. We want a clean victory, good winning over bad, with no nasties lurking on the sideline."

Mallory nodded, his mind racing electrically at what the Supreme Commander had just told him.

"Okay, Commander, we know roughly which way the Melmer shipment is heading. Our experts have made a rough guess at its size and the number of troops guarding it. They're from the survivors of the SS defence of Berlin. They've got Frogs, Belgies, Cheeseheads and Krauts guarding their precious Führer – renegades from half of Europe. But to guard the Melmer shipment, they've got the survivors of SS Assault Regiment Wotan. You know the guy and the tough hombres he commands."

Mallory certainly did. They had nearly put paid to his own little group of toughs and old lags at Trier three months before. They were, as the Supreme Commander, an addict of cowboy novels, had called them, "tough hombres". "Yes I know them sir," Malloy confirmed wearily.

"Well, you can reckon on half a hundred of them at least. But whatever their number I want all of them – I repeat, *all* of them, wiped from the face of this earth." Now Mallory could really see the desperate, almost demented look on Ike's face. It was that of a man nearly at the end of his tether. "Dead men tell no tales. Clear?"

"Yessir."

"I'm going to give you half a company of General Gavin's 'All-Americans' to help you. You'll have no time to bring up your own fellers. Gavin's airborne troopers are fine soldiers.

Like all of their kind, they're out for war and women. They won't ask any questions. And that's as it should be."

Mallory waited. Already Patton was waving excitedly at Eisenhower, crying, "Get a gander at this, Ike. Just look at this dame's tits, willya!" Mallory knew what was coming, but still he waited.

Then it came. Now Eisenhower was vastly formal: "Commander Mallory, I never want to hear of the Melmer shipment again. It has to disappear from the face of the earth as if it had never existed. That's all. Good luck. Dismiss." With that he turned and started back to an excited Patton, saying, "Georgie, willya keep your voice down? One day that voice is gonna ruin yer . . ."

Three

"Cavalry," von Dodenburg said, lowering his glasses. "Red Cavalry!" "Cossacks, *Gospodin*," the little *Hiwi* sergeant standing next to von Dodenburg and Hackmann in the turret of the Renault tank corrected the tall blond SS officer. "I smell them . . . Cossacks stink of shit." He showed that glistening mouthful of stainless steel teeth, as if it was all an excellent joke.

It wasn't for Hackmann. The pudgy *Standartenführer* with the pince-nez paled. "Oh my God, they tell some horrible tales about the Cossacks. My father told me about them when he was in Russia in the First World War."

"*Da, nyet horoscho*," the *Hiwi* agreed, as if he were support- ing the frightened SS officer, "they stick wood up arse . . . chop hands off," he lowered his voice, "cut tail off Fritz soldier." He leered at Hackmann: "Horrible!"

Von Dodenburg grinned at Hackmann's all too obvious funk. The slimy swine would be filling his pants any moment now. Kuno could actually smell his overwhelming abject fear.

They had escaped the Russian Stormoviks. The planes had buzzed the Wotan's hiding place several times, but in the end they had given up attempting to find the German column and had flown off in search of other targets – the Brandenburg countryside was full of escaping German units heading south for the supposed safety of the Alps. But the Cavalry was something different; they couldn't be thrown off so easily. They'd spotted the Germans and would stay with them until air came up or they attacked themselves. It was up to him, von Dodenburg, to find some way of getting rid of the riders before air arrived. On that broad plain, devoid of good hiding places, they'd be sitting ducks.

"But we're armour," Hackmann protested. "We've got artillery and armoured protection. I can't see what those half-civilised Russian brutes over there can do against us, von Dodenburg."

"You'd be surprised," Kuno answered, pondering the new situation thoughtfully. He could see the Cossacks were employing their usual strategy. They were extending their lines and trying to outpace the armoured column, moving slowly at the speed of the heavily laden Melmer trucks. Once they'd extended the "horn", as it was called, to the front of the column, they'd use it for delaying tactics: ambushes, sudden charges, which were usually feints, and the like. By slowing the column they'd make the Germans *laager* for the night – and then the real fireworks would commence.

"How?"

"At nightfall, *Standartenführer*, all our heavy weapons and armour are useless. The Cossacks are past masters at infiltration."

The little *Hiwi* nodded his agreement. With a dirty forefinger and a huge steel gleaming grin, he drew a line across his throat, as if he were slitting it.

Hackmann gave a shudder.

"Yes, that sort of thing. And what good is a thick piece of armour plating against some Ivan peasant armed with a rocket projector? In the darkness we'd be helpless to stop them." He added his own grin to that of the Russian turncoat. It did him good to see the SS official squirm with fear.

Hackmann took a grip on himself. "But then what are you going to do to stop the fiends?" he demanded. "After all, it is your duty to ensure that the Melmer shipment gets through, come what may. Those are *Reichsleiter* Bormann's express orders, remember, von Dodenburg? May I remind you of that?"

"And may I remind you, *Standartenführer* Hackmann," Kuno said with mock severity, "*Reichsleiter* Bormann is in

Berlin and we're here out in the field, relying totally on our own talents and experience." He looked across at Hackmann, who was suddenly not only very frightened, but totally deflated, as if he was realising for the first time that he was out of his depth on the battlefield, and that all the power he had once exercised from behind a desk meant nothing now.

"However, *Standartenführer*, all is not lost," von Dodenburg continued. "We've experienced this kind of situation before. We know how to tackle it." Even as he said the words so confidently, von Dodenburg gave a silent prayer to heaven that he did. He pressed his throat mike. "Schulze," he called. "Do you read me, Sergeant Schulze?"

Matz was squatted on the top of his Renault's deck, cleaning his yellowed, filthy toenails with the tip of his bayonet, while opposite him Schulze sipped moodily at his last flatman of schnapps. They had, of course, seen the Cossack scouts on the skyline, silhouetted a stark black against the afternoon sun. But the sight hadn't worried them particularly; they'd seen Cossack scouts before. Matz had just turfed out a particularly obstinate piece of muck from his big toenail, when in the turret, the young radio operator pulled one earphone to the side and called, "Sarge – it's for you."

"*Sarge!*" Schulze feigned mock rage. "Do my shell-like ears deceive me? That cardboard Christmas tree soldier just called me 'Sarge'. Snap a sergeant-major on it, laddie, or else you'll get the tip of my dicebeaker" – by which he meant his jackboot – "up yer keester so hard that yer eyes'll pop out of yer skull!"

The radio operator paled under the terrible threat, added the necessary rank and handed the earphones over to Schulze speedily, as if they were red-hot and burning his hands. Schulze listened intently. Then he pressed the throat mike and barked in a very businesslike way, at least for him: "Understood, *Obersturm*. Will be done. Over and out."

He levered himself out of the turret hastily and glared at Matz, who had finished with his toenails and was now loosening his belt in preparation for the more intimate cleaning operation at the bottom end of his abdomen, saying, "I wonder if I should clean my bayonet first. I don't want to catch anything down there."

Schulze laughed scornfully at his old comrade and snapped, "You ain't got nothing down there to worry about in the first place. Now put that pig-sticker away and look a bit decent. *Dalli . . . dalli.*"

Obediently, Matz did as he was commanded before asking, "And what, mastermind, does the Old Man want us to do?"

Schulze breathed in an affected way on his hand, as if he were some society woman drying her recently painted nails. "Just a social call on our dear Russian comrades. A dish of tea, a smidgen of caviar perhaps, and a couple of goblets of champers. That sort of thing," he said in what he regarded as a high-faluting voice before exploding, "What in three devils' name do yer think we're gonna do, arse-with-ears! We're gonna nobble a couple of frigging hairy-assed Ivans. Now get yer frigid digit out of yer frigging orifice. *MOVE!*"

Matz moved.

Now the sun was beginning to sink. Long shadows spread across the intervening pasture, as the two columns, cavalry and armour, continued on their steady route southwards. But the sun was to the advantage of the two men who had just dropped into the dead ground from the passing Renault light tank. It was streaming in at an oblique angle, blinding the Cossack observers. With luck, Schulze told himself as they began to move out, it would blind and bedazzle the Russians until they were within snatching distance of their victims.

As von Dodenburg had hurriedly briefed them, "I don't want any heroes, dead or otherwise, you two rogues. I want live cowards with prisoners. We've got to know what the Ivans know and if they have any orders from higher up."

"How do you mean, sir?" Schulze had asked hurriedly, as he had stuck stick grenades in his jackboots, and checked that he had his "Hamburger Equaliser" and razor-sharp special combat bayonet.

"Are they just an ordinary marauding Cossack patrol? You

know what they're like, Schulze. Out for loot and hot gash, as you would say."

"Nothing against hot gash, save it's wasted on the Russkis," Schulze had interjected.

"Or are they specifically looking for us on account of you know what," von Dodenburg had continued, indicating the lumbering trucks carrying the Melmer gold. "For if they are, we're in bad trouble. So, you heroes, bring me back live Russians with lively tongues. Don't attempt to fight a private battle against the glorious Red Army."

Now, Matz didn't need a second invitation. "I'm off," he responded immediately to Schulze's monosyllabic command. He darted forward, the strap of his wooden leg creaking audibly, as he advanced a few paces, dropped and, jerking up his machine pistol, covered Schulze who was going to perform the "snatch", whenever they came within kidnapping distance of some poor Cossack who wouldn't know what was going to hit him.

As Matz lay there, gasping a little, his nostrils were assailed by a strange fetid animal smell which he couldn't quite make out. It wasn't the customary Cossack stink of black *marhokka* tobacco, garlic, stale human sweat and horseshit; it was something different. But what? He raised his head and sniffed the air, his nostrils twitching like that of an animal himself. No luck. He couldn't make it out. In the end he gave up and whistled softly.

It was the signal.

For such a big man, Schulze moved with remarkable quietness. He stole by Matz's covering position in the hollow like some grey silent predatory animal, seeking out its prey. A few moments later he had vaulted a rough wooden fence and disappeared into what appeared to be a tumbledown barn next to the long burrow, what the farmers called a "pie", in which they stored the turnips for their animals' winter feed.

Carefully, making himself do so slowly, Matz counted off the seconds, until Schulze would signal that he had wormed inside the burrow, composed of layer upon layer of turnips, covered by straw and topped by soil. Finally it came, yet another low whistle.

Matz raised himself and stopped dead, body pressed against the nearest tree trunk, head bent back so as not to give him away. A lone Russian, bowlegged like all cavalrymen, was leading his horse by the reins. But he wasn't alone. Behind him trotted a couple of dogs. Matz whistled softly to himself and then cursed when he recognised them for what they were. He froze.

Schulze, from his hiding place, must have made the same discovery in that exact same instant. For suddenly he threw back the mixture of soil, straw and turnips in a small eruption that startled the cavalryman so much that he let loose of the horse and the two rough, hairy hounds, with the strange contraptions strapped on their backs. Puzzled by the strange apparition, the dogs didn't even bark. As for the Cossack, he was so shaken by Schulze that his tall, rakishly tilted fur hat fell off. For an instant, a watching, tense Matz thought he was going to be fool enough to pick it up. Then, realising the danger he was in, the Cossack grabbed for the carbine slung across his shoulders.

Schulze reacted. He reached for a grenade. The Cossack was quicker, firing first. The slug howled off the side of the barn, showering Schulze with an angry burst of wood splinters.

"Ferk this for a game o' soldiers!" Schulze yelled and dropped to the ground instinctively. He knew that Matz was covering him.

The latter didn't hesitate. His lips writhing angrily, he levelled his machine pistol and pressed the trigger. "Try this on for frigging collar size!" he yelled, as the gun erupted at his right shoulder.

The Cossack reacted just as quickly. Fire stabbed the shadows. All around Matz the earth erupted, and something hit him a stinging blow in the face. He'd had enough. He reached in his boot, and in one and the same moment, pulled out the stick grenade, jerked the china pin and then flung it with all his strength in the lone Cossack's direction.

In a fury of flame, it exploded. The Cossack's mount reared up on its hindlegs. The Cossack reeled backwards, his face gone, what looked like molten red wax dripping down from the gleaming white bones thereby revealed. The dogs broke loose. In the very same instant that the Cossack, writhing and threshing in his death throes, finally succumbed to his fate, they started to pelt towards the long line of slow-moving German vehicles on the horizon. With grim purposeful determination they hurried to their victims.

Four

"*Boshe moi,*" the *Hiwi* sergeant gasped and crossed himself hastily in the elaborate Russian fashion.

"What is it?" von Dodenburg yelled above the roar of the tank engine churning across the plain in one of the low gears.

"Look!" the terrified little NCO with the stainless steel teeth hissed. He flung out his hand.

Von Dodenburg followed the direction he indicated. Two small shapes coming in from left and right were heading for the German convoy, going all out, while behind them the Cossacks had remounted and drawn their sabres, almost as if they were going to charge the enemy armour.

"What's going on—" he started to say, but von Dodenburg never finished his question. The *Hiwi* supplied the answer first: "Dogs," he cried, "the Cossack swine are using battle dogs."

The blond, harshly handsome SS Colonel gasped. He hadn't encountered battle dogs for years now. He thought the Russians had given them up. They had a never-ending source of manpower, after all, and men were easier to train than dogs. Obviously, he had been wrong. Here, the Ivans were using them again. Suddenly, startlingly, he realised the danger they were in. Hastily he pressed the throat mike. "To all," he rapped. "Battle dogs on both flanks. Shoot on sight. Blast them off the face of the earth, *NOW*—" The rest of his almost panic-stricken command was drowned out by the sound of the gunner opening up.

BRRR! Like the sound of an angry woodpecker, the Renault's Hotchkiss machine gun scythed the air to the little tank's front. White and red tracer streaked towards the nearest dog, which was gathering speed by the instant.

Von Dodenburg flung up his glass, panting as if he were running a fast race. The nearest dog was still going all out. Its ugly snout was kept low, its ears clipped down against its long skull. But it was the horn of its back and the heavy package on both sides of its flanks on which von Dodenburg concentrated as the ugly dog slid silently into the twin circles of calibrated glass. He knew the dog's tactic of old. Once below the line of defensive fire – for the turret could only be depressed a certain amount – it would make that final all-out dash and squeeze beneath the tank, as it had been trained to do. Then they would have had it. Once that horn touched a bogie or track, it would detonate the two cases of high explosive and in an instant they'd be on their way to having tea and creamcakes with the angels.

He bit his teeth into his bottom lip with repressed tension until he tasted blood, and willed the gunner to knock out the first dog. It was within a hundred metres of so of their tank. A couple more and it would be below the gunner's arc of fire, and after that he didn't dare think the terrible thought through to its final conclusion.

Up near their hiding place, Schulze and Matz were undecided. They looked at the dead Russian sprawled out in the unnatural grotesque position of those done violently to death, and then at the Russian cavalry preparing to mount. Already the Cossack ensigns, brilliant in their traditional skirt coats with the gold cartridge pouches across their breasts, gleaming ancient sabres dangling from their belts, had begun to move out. Further back, the enormously fat *Hetman*, the Cossack chief, was waddling to his own sturdy white stallion, assisted by two young cavalrymen, and followed by his flag bearer, carrying the traditional black skull and crossbones of the marauding Cossack tribe.

"What d'yer think, Matzi?" Schulze hissed as they crouched there, watching the cavalrymen.

"Well, yer don't need a crystal ball, Schulze," his old

running mate answered, whispering too. "They're gonna wait till those bloody hounds get among the column, then they're gonna charge. They'll hope our lads'll be disorganised by then and they'll get in and among the armour, before they can use their turret peashotters."

"*Genau*," Schulze said. "But what can we do?" he added miserably. To their left the Cossacks were releasing yet more of the battle dogs, real brutes, half Husky, half Alsatian. "So it's gonna have to be us against the Cossacks after all," he added with forced contempt.

"Well, we can't stop those shitting hounds, that's for sure," Matz concluded in agreement. "So it's got to be the cavalry. After all, they're only armed with them toothpicks of theirs. Even a barnshitter like you, Schulze, weak on the breast, as you are, could manage that lot."

Schulze muttered an impossible to carry out threat under his breath and said, "Come on, then. Do you heroes want to live for frigging ever? It's got to be that frigging fat *Hetman* of theirs, hasn't it?"

Sadly Matz concluded it had to be. They started to crawl forward for a few metres. They paused in a small dip in the ground to observe the fat commander waiting till his escort steadied his mount. All the same, the *Hetman* did not relinquish his antique silver sabre, which had probably been handed down for centuries. The sight made Matz shudder a little. Apprehensively he took his metal shaving mirror from the breast pocket of his tunic and stuffed it down beneath his flies. "Yer never know with them Cossacks," he told himself, "they'd whip a man's tail off with them toothpicks o' theirs quicker than the Chief Rabbi docks a poor old Jew's dick!"

They crawled on . . .

Meanwhile, the gunner on von Dodenburg's tank sweated with frustration. The dog was only metres away. He had depressed his gun to its lowest level. Now the tracer was striking the ground all about the racing beast, intent now on getting under the tank as it had been trained to do so. In a minute it would be too late. Next to von Dodenburg and the

Hiwi, a frantic Hackmann clamoured for the tank to stop. "For heaven's sake, let's bale out while we've still got time," he shrieked, face contorted with overwhelming unreasoning fear. "*PLEASE*!"

Von Dodenburg ignored him. He had other things to do. He had snatched the *Hiwi*'s machine pistol and now, steadying himself the best he could in the swaying turret, he was adding his own fire to that of the Renault's gunner.

Suddenly the gunner stopped firing. His tracer was now zipping useless above the racing dog's head. Hackmann screamed. He covered his face like a hysterical woman. "Save me," he yelled. "Oh please God . . . save me, won't you, God . . ."

Von Dodenburg elbowed him out of the way roughly. He took aim, steadying himself and his breathing, for it was now or never. The dog of death was a mere ten metres or so away. It was already slowing down, as it eyed the tracks, readying to find a way under them as it had been trained to do. Mud and pebbles splattered its ugly snout and head. They didn't deter it. In a moment it would be all over. Hackman started to wet himself with fear. He was going to die, die now after all the work he had put into his plan, the risks he had run. Heaven, arse and cloudburst, it wasn't fair.

Von Dodenburg pressed his trigger. He clenched his teeth savagely, almost like a wild beast himself, and kept his forefinger down hard. Tracer stabbed the afternoon gloom. The air was filled with the stink of explosive. Still the dog came on, the white tracer zipping uselessly over its skull.

Suddenly, startlingly, it happened: the animal faltered in mid stride. A great scarlet patch began to spread rapidly on its flank. Still von Dodenburg didn't relax his pressure on the trigger, as the dog began to slow. Its head fell. Gamely, it tried to continue. Too late. The whole dog rose abruptly in a burst of vivid scarlet flame. Next moment it disintegrated as both containers of high explosive went up with a tremendous roar that seemed to go on and on for ever.

In the turret they ducked hastily. Blood and gore splashed

everywhere. A head slammed against the side of the tank. A severed leg whacked a sobbing, hysterical Hackmann across the face. He went out like a light. Next moment it was all over and the Renault was surging forward, dripping bright red blood, a hindleg caught in its track moving up and down, as if waving goodbye . . .

Schulze breathed out hard. "Christ, I nearly pissed in my boot," he gasped at the close call.

"*Nearly*!" Matz echoed. "My boot's full of frigging urine—" he broke off abruptly. The *Hetman* had finally managed to mount his stallion, the animal sagging visibly under his tremendous weight. Behind the two observers, the first dog was seen to be successful. One of the Melmer trucks rose into the air. Next moment, it slammed down again, its rear axle smashed and smoking, gold bars leaking from beneath the torn, scorched canvas.

Both of the old hares forced themselves to concentrate on the Cossacks. They feared the worse for their comrades left behind in the column. The dogs were everywhere now. But they knew the Old Man would do his best to keep the casualties down. Now it was up to them to deflect the Cossacks, make them retreat and take with them their damned dogs. But what could they do, just two men armed with handguns, against a whole Cossack regiment?

Schulze thought he knew the answer. "The fat prick," he said, and indicated the *Hetman* who was now watching the dogs through an old-fashioned telescope, while behind him, a young blond ensign was adjusting the black flag pole in the stirrup cup to the right of his highly burnished saddle.

"Do you think we could pick him off and get away with it, Schulze?" Matz asked hesitantly.

"What do you think, birdbrain?" Schulze snorted. "We have to try – soon. There's no other choice."

"If they charged—"

"They will," Schulze cut him off sharply. "Look, they're bringing up their band. When they do charge, that's our only real chance. Knock off their *Hetman* and take off in the confusion." *If you're lucky, old house*, a small voice at the back of his mind admonished Schulze.

The band dismounted, shuffling into a hasty semblance of the position of attention. The drum major raised his baton. The last of the afternoon sun gleamed on the polished brass as the bandsmen raised their instruments. The drum major's baton came down stiffly across his proud peacock chest. There was a blare of brass, the rattle of kettledrums. A snappy march erupted, with Schulze breathing in awe, "Well, I live and breathe, Matzi. Did you ever see anything like it?" Matz had to admit that he had not.

With difficulty the Cossack *Hetman* raised himself from his saddle. The old stallion seemed to bend under his weight. He thrust up his sabre. It gleamed a bright silver. He waved it three times above his fur cap. A great roar went up from the mass ranks of the horsemen. To their front the dogs were now among the Fritz vehicles. Here and there wrecked trucks were already burning. There were ragged, gory remains of dead hounds everywhere. Still the survivors tried to wriggle themselves under the trucks.

Schulze began to take aim. Next to him, Matz pulled the detonating pin out of a smoke grenade. It was the only way he could think of covering their retreat – if they survived to do so.

Schulze took first pressure. The fat *Hetman* was dissected by the metal crossbars of his sights. He felt the damp sweat began to trickle down the small of his back. A nerve started to tick at his temple. He forced himself to be calm. He controlled his breathing with great difficulty. In a minute, he knew, his nerve would run away with him.

The *Hetman* yelled an order. Half a thousand voices yelled in bass chorus, "*Slava Cossaki!*" There was something awesome in that great spectacle as the band blared and the flagbearer raised his black flag. Slowly, in perfect formation, the riders started to move off. The *Hetman* shouldered his gleaming silver sabre. Despite his grossness there seemed something heroic about him, too. The walk started to give way to a canter. The cavalrymen began to rise and sink in their saddles. They were getting closer now. Schulze took second pressure. Next to him Matz could have shouted madly with the absolute tension of it all. Behind them yet another truck came to an abrupt halt and burst into flames.

Matz's nerves tingled. The strain was unbearable. Why didn't Schulze, the big shit, pull his trigger and get it over with? They weren't going to survive anyway. How could they, against a whole regiment of Ivan cavalry? They might as well snuff it here and now.

But Schulze wasn't to be rushed. He had to knock the *Hetman* out. As always with the Russians, even with the Cossack, if you knocked out their leader, they went to pieces for a while until they got another one to give them orders. The Soviet Workers Paradise had brainwashed them too long into a tame submission where it was highly dangerous to make your own decisions. You ended in the gulag – or worse – if you did. He sucked the butt of his machine pistol into his shoulder more tightly and started to count off the seconds: "*Three, two . . .*"

Now the canter was speeding up. Soon the flag and that silver sabre would point forward along the horses' flying manes and they would go into that final dicing with death, the charge. Schulze knew the time had come.

"*THREE!*" he bellowed aloud and pulled the trigger.

Things happened with tremendous speed now. The weapon slammed into his shoulder. Fire spat from the muzzle. Up front, the *Hetman* seemed to raise himself even higher from his gleaming ornate saddle. Next to him the young ensign carrying the flag looked puzzled, almost foolishly so. The flag dropped from an abruptly nerveless hand. Slowly but surely the ensign started to slither down the side of his white mare, while behind him the Cossack riders stared uncomprehendingly, waiting for the order to charge.

Schulze hit the trigger again. A vicious burst ripped along the front rank of the horsemen as the *Hetman*, still firm in the saddle, slumped dead over the mane of his horse. Men went down everywhere. Horses too, whinnying and shrieking, flail-

"Naturally, merely a few dozen young men."

But irony was wasted on the *Standartenführer*, who continued, "The question is now this: how quickly can the convoy move with this extra weight, and what is our best route southwards, now the damned Reds have spotted us?"

Von Dodenburg pretended to consider his question seriously. In fact he wasn't one bit interested in the treasure or their route, as long as it was safe from attack. All that mattered to him now was getting as many of his young troopers through safely to the south. Then, once the surrender came, which it surely would soon, he wanted to discharge them – he had come prepared with the necessary documentation and stamps – and have them avoid the misery and indignity of the POW camps. "Have you any suggestions, *Standartenführer*?" he countered, giving himself more time to reflect upon the problem.

It was the chance that Hackmann had been waiting for ever since the Russians had discovered them, when he had concluded that his original plan was in danger. "Yes," he answered promptly, pulling himself together. "You know our destinaton?"

"*Jawohl, Standartenführer*," von Dodenburg answered, suddenly suspicious at the bureaucrat's speedy response. Normally, frigging glorified clerks and rear echelon stallions like Hackmann took ages to make up their minds. Their slowness to make decisions went with the job, von Dodenburg guessed. "*Reichsleiter* Bormann instructed that we should make for Berchtesgaden for posting to the Alpine Fortress once we had delivered the Melmer shipment," he barked authoritatively.

"There is no Alpine Fortress," Hackmann snapped. "It's a figment of our own propaganda and the fears of those weak-kneed Anglo-Americans. We have troops there, up in the mountains, but no fortifications have been built and no troops have been allotted to defend those non-existent fortifications," he ended with a sneer, hoping he had taken this arrogant young man with his damned decorations and handsome mug down a peg or two.

Admittedly von Dodenburg was surprised by Hackmann's disclosure. The thought of the Alpine Fortress where the cream of the German Army might hold out for years, wearing the Allies down sufficently so that they would offer a beaten Germany a better peace than unconditional surrender, had kept many loyal Germans such as himself going. All the same, he could now see some chance for the Regiment in the fact that there was not in fact a last-ditch defensive position which they would be honour-bound, due to their SS oath of loyalty, to defend to the grave. Now Wotan had the freedom to do what it wished, either to save itself or to destroy itself. He tried to keep the sudden knowledge that they were almost free at last from his face. Instead, he said carefully, "I see, *Standartenführer*. So what do you suggest?"

Hackmann hesitated only a fraction of a second before responding. "We head for a totally different destination. We can be sure," he said, and indicated the shattered corpses of the dogs everywhere, "that the damned Reds know about us. That message Bormann sent us – and here von Dodenburg noted the "Bormann" without the rank of "*Reichsleiter*": which meant that Hackmann was finished with his former boss – "has probably also been picked up by the Western Allies. I've always suspected for years now that they picked up all our radio messages, even at the highest level." He shrugged carelessly. "No matter. It's too late now."

"Our new destination?" von Dodenburg persisted.

"The home of the movement," Hackmann said.

"The home of the movement," von Dodenburg echoed. "You mean Nuremberg?"

Hackmann nodded, eyeing the younger SS officer carefully as if he were trying to assess his reaction to the news.

Nuremberg had long been celebrated throughout the National Socialist Party as the place where the Führer had held the Party's annual rallies, even in the days before he had actually come to power. Hence its name throughout the Reich. "But why there?" von Dodenburg asked, puzzled.

Hackmann grinned, revealing a mouthful of yellow tomb-stone-like teeth, flecked here and there with gold in the middle-class fashion. Typical small town stuff, Kuno told himself, but still he made no comment. He was too eager to hear Hackmann's reasons for his choice.

Hackmann let him wait, however.

Simultaneously, out in the field, the burial party was bringing in the last of the corpses for the mass burial pit. Carefully, two corporals searched the shattered bodies for ammunition and the like, while Sergeant Major Schulze kept a wary eye open. It was his "bounden duty to confiscate any offensive items", as he proclaimed. By that the big ex-docker meant contraceptives, dirty French pictures, and more importantly "cancer sticks" and "firewater".

"Can't let that kind of poison fall into the hands of our clean-living youths of Wotan," Schultze reflected thoughtfully.

Hackmann, meanwhile, answered his own question: "Because there is still a group of individuals there who are one hundred per cent for our cause and who will help us, come what may. There are no turncoats there like there have been in Aachen and Cologne, I can assure you of that, *Obersturmbannführer*."

"Very well. But what have they got to do with us?" Kuno asked slowly, a thought beginning to uncurl unpleasantly in his mind, as he began to realise what Hackmann's true intention was.

"Naturally, Nuremberg is on the Allies' line of advancement into Bavaria from the west and the rest of their forces coming up through Italy. But Berchtesgaden is obviously the glittering prize for them. Their *Ami* generals will want the kudos and naturally the newspaper headlines of being the conquerors of Berchtesgaden. So it stands to reason that they will not waste any time on Nuremburg if the defenders put up a spirited defence, of which," – he smiled confidently at a thoughtful von Dodenburg – "you can be assured they will."

Von Dodenburg grunted unintelligibly, but otherwise made no direct comment.

"At Nuremberg, von Dodenburg, our friends of the new *Werewolf* will assist us on the final stage of our long journey," Hackmann beamed and threw out his pigeon chest proudly. "And I can safely say that the men and women of the *Werewolf* will brook no opposition. If anyone is going to see us through, it will be them. Now, I suggest, von Dodenburg, that we finish cleaning up. The most important thing, the Melmer shipment, has been taken care of. We ought to be on our way." He looked at the darkening sky and, seemingly suddenly afraid, he shivered and said in a strange, unreal voice, "I think a louse just ran over my liver, von Dodenburg." And with that he was gone back to the tank.

"Louse over his frigging liver," Schulze grunted, just catching the last of the conversation. "Let's hope the bugger was wearing hobnailed ammo boots." Generously, he offered a puzzled, reflective von Dodenburg a full packet of "*Juno Eckstien*". "Lung torpedo, sir? Take the lot. Plenty more where that came from." He winked knowingly. "Whipped it out of his nibs' kit when he wasn't looking."

Kuno forced a smile and said, "You big rogue, you are well known for your thieving ways and your intimacy with the mind of the criminal classes."

Schulze beamed broadly at what he took to be praise, for in truth he had not altogether understood the "Old Man".

"So, have you ever heard of something called the *Werewolf*? And I don't mean those old horror films from the UFA?" By this von Dodenburg meant the Berlin film studios of their distant youth.

Schulze frowned. "I have, sir."

"Well, what is it – or what are they?"

"A lot of wet-assed young kids from the Hitler Youth and the Association of German Maidens," – here he gave a passing leer at the name – "so-called. They've been trained by some of our comrades for stay-behind roles. You know: spying, sabotage and the like."

Kuno whistled softly. "You mean partisans like those the Ivans have? That kind of nasty business?"

Schulze nodded solemnly. He took out his looted flatman and took a great swig of the fiery liquid, his Adam's apple racing up and down his throat like an express lift. He coughed, wiped the back of his big paw across hairy lips, before continuing, "Plain suicide, if you ask me, sir – for *our* side."

"But why does Hackmann want to risk the treasure and his own damned skinny neck by placing it all in the hands of a bunch of young fanatics in short pants, Schulze?" von Dodenburg asked a little desperately.

Schulze remained silent. For once, the man who had an answer for everything, had none.

Part Three
Dangerous Youth

"Führer, command – we follow!"
Motto of the Hitler Youth

One

Wheels! It was as if the whole of Central Germany – Mecklenburg, Brandenburg, Saxony – was on the move. Everything
that possessed wheels had been pressed into service. There
were petrolless old Opels, pulled by horses, oxen towing
long columns of what looked like prairie schooners, with
smoking chimneys poking through their makeshift tarpaulin
roofs, and tractors pulling haywagons, packed with sobbing
children and toothless old crones, swaying back and forth,
as if in some strange oriental ritual. There were women with
rucksacks pushing piled-high wickerwork children's buggies,
even wheelbarrows wobbling and swaying under monstrous
loads. Wheels were at a premium this last week of April
1945.

"But where in Sam Hill are they going, Commander?"
Lieutenant Grogan of the US 82nd Airborne Division – the
"All American" – asked, as they paused yet again and let
another frightened column of refugees cross the road before
they headed northwards once more.

Mallory pushed his battered old naval cap to the back of
his head and wiped the opaque pearls of sweat from his
forehead. It was very hot for the time of year. "Search me,
Grogan," he answered, half-puzzled, half-angry at being
delayed yet once again. "What gets in people when they
panic? Hell, you know," he said as he looked at the US
paratrooper with his two purple hearts and silver para wings,
liking what he saw – Grogan was a veteran of Normandy,
Holland and Bastogne – "you've seen it all before. Unlike
your chaps." He indicated the paratroopers, all fresh-faced

boys in spite of their tough appearance, who had never been in action before.

The teenage soldiers, who had been fetched from the US Airborne depot in France, were staring at the refugees wide-eyed. They were making the usual cracks, mostly sexual, holding out Hershey bars to the more attractive German women and crying in broken German, "*Du schlafen mir . . . Schokolade?*" But it was clear that they were bemused and perhaps even a little upset by what they saw. They had never featured this kind of panicked misery in the Hollywood war movies on which they had been brought up.

Grogan gave a tired snort, his mouth relaxing into a crooked grin in that confident Texan manner of his. Mallory told himself that *Grogan* would never panic.

The young American officer was going to be just the man he needed, once they left the main thrust of the US Armies moving southwards, and commenced their trek north to stop these mysterious Huns who had recently escaped from the Bunker and were attempting to make a break for it.

"Real outlaw country," Grogan commented and signalled to his young soldiers that they should cease calling out to the harassed German civilians. "All we need just now is John Wayne as a waggon train boss," he laughed drily.

Mallory smiled momentarily and then his scarred face hardened once more. "All right, they're thinning out now. Tell your chaps to mount up again, we've got to get cracking."

"Get cracking?" Grogan quizzed, mimicking the English accent and expression before calling, "OK, you guys, haul ass! Saddle up – move it out, *now*!"

There were the usual moans and protests which Mallory had become accustomed to hearing from American troops when their officers gave them orders, but the young paras "moved it" quickly enough!

Behind Mallory, Spiv said to Thaelmann, speaking loud enough for the Commander to hear, quite deliberately so, "Load of old rubbish. Why the boss wants them Yanks, I don't know. Bunch of bed-wetters, if ever I saw one. We could handle this little lot of Jerries with one frigging hand behind our backs." He spat contemptuously into the white dust of the country road.

Thaelmann took his hard, fanatical gaze off a woman, well advanced in pregnancy, who was walking past with difficulty, holding her swollen stomach tenderly as if she might give birth at any moment. He felt sympathy – after all, they were his own people. "But when the times were good, they went along with Hitler," he told himself. "Now they'll have to suffer."

"Come on, d'yer want a special invite?" Spiv urged. "We ain't got all day."

Thaelmann gave the smaller man that permanently angry puce-faced look of his which frightened most people – though not the little ex-cockney barrow boy – and hissed, "Don't hurry me, Spiv. I am thinking."

"Save it for when yer having a sly, crafty wank in the bog, mate. Move!"

Five minutes later the little convoy of five halftracks, led by Mallory's jeep, was jolting its way north again. Above them the clouds were coming in grey and sullen. It looked as if they were in for a storm. Behind them, on the wooded hill, the signal lamp started to blink on and off urgently . . .

That day they covered twenty miles. Whilst the black clouds above became ever more threatening and in the distance the lightning zig-zagged in silent crimson flashes above the hills, the little convoy progressed ever deeper into "outlaw country," as Grogan called it. But even the Marauders, experts at this kind of long distance penetration, could not detect any outlaws. Apart from the occasional "trek", as the Germans apparently called the columns of refugees heading southwards into the unknown, the countryside seemed deserted.

All the same, Mallory, riding in the back of the jeep with Grogan in the front seat next to Thaelmann, who was doing the driving, felt a sense of unease. He could not truly reason why, but he knew that he felt watched, and more than once he flung a glance over his shoulder, as if he half-expected something unpleasant to be there. But all he saw was a line of US White halftracks, filled with sleepy paras. Otherwise, there was nothing to be seen.

About four that April afternoon, with the rain beginning to come down in fitful little stops and starts, the storm finally broke. Now the thunder was directly above. Roll after roll of booming noise echoed across the landscape in between the electric flashes of lightning, and soon the rain started to fall out of the heavens in a solid grey sheet.

For a while the little convoy continued. But finally Mallory was forced to tell himself that it was no use continuing with the men getting drenched in the open vehicles. Besides, the young paras had not eaten anything but cold K-rations since dawn, and his own stomach was beginning to growl in anticipation of warm food, even if it were the K-rations' nauseatingly greasy pork and beans. It was time to find shelter.

They didn't take long to find it. In the distance, wiping their faces and eyes constantly against the onslaught of beating cold rain the four of them in the jeep made out a collection of half-timbered houses on the road some half a mile in front of them. Grogan pulled out his carbine from the leather bucket holster next to his seat, clicked off the handy little weapon's safety and ordered Thaelmann to "hit the gas, soldier. But keep your eyes peeled."

"Like tinned tomatoes, sir," Spiv, sitting next to Mallory, cried cheekily: something which earned him a frown of disapproval from a soaked Commander Mallory.

They slowed down as they approached the cluster of old houses, huddled around the typical onion-roofed Baroque church of the area. Grogan waved his hand around his helmet and then placed his fingers outspread on top of it.

Spiv pulled a face at the signal. But Mallory approved: Grogan was playing it exactly right. The place looked harmless enough, and the men were soaked and weary, but all the same he was not going to take chances that they might be ambushed.

While the second and third halftrack turned left and right,

crossing the drainage ditches at the side of the country road, heading for the flanks and rear exit to the village, the men of the first vehicle clattered over to where Grogen was standing, carbine in his hands.

Swiftly and precisely, as if he had done it plenty of times before, the young para officer snapped out his orders. "Joe, you with me. Al and Hank up with 'Ole Sarge'." "Ole Sarge" was all of nineteen. "Okay, let's go, guys," the youngster confirmed.

Even Spiv was impressed. "Don't half move fast, them Yanks," he said to Thaelmann.

Thaelmann, the old school German communist, grunted. "Typical products of capitalist society. Move or you're out of work."

Mallory shook his head in mock sadness. Old *Trautgott* – "Trust God" – Thaelmann would never learn. Stalin, the communist dictator, was just as bad as Hitler. But that meant nothing to the German Red. His mind had been fixed for all time, back in his communist youth days in Altona, Hamburg. He dismissed the Marauder: "All right, we'll play the innocent Fairy Queen. Move it, Thaelmann."

The jeep started to move forward slowly, making a tempting target for anyone hidden in the old houses, while Spiv sang, seemingly happily, under his breath, "*Tight as a drum . . . Never been done . . . Queen of all the Fairies. Ain't it a pity she's only one titty to feed the baby . . . Poor little bugger he's only got one udder.*" At this point Mallory, his nerves jingling ever so slightly with the tension, hissed, "All right, Caruso, put a sock in it."

Obediently, Spiv did just that.

Up front, Grogan and his little squad proceeded along either side of the street, weapons at the ready, eyes flashing from roof to road, kicking open the doors of the houses, diving in, ready to open fire at the first sign of the enemy. It was all very professional, Mallory thought, but still smacked of the training school. Grogan's men were raw. They should have gone down the street like a dose of salts, not giving the

Germans time to prepare themselves for their attackers. The whole essence of house-to-house combat was to catch the defender off-guard. Still, Grogan was doing well with what was available. He now pulled up and slipped his pistol from inside his belt – keeping it in holster only slowed up the action. "All right, the two of you," he commanded. "Move out and see what you can find. I'll check the steeple tower of the church. And Spiv," he added.

"Sir?"

"No loot or rapine. Remember we represent the King-Emperor," he warned, face set in an assumed serious look.

"Sir. You can rely on old Spiv to bear the honour of the King-Emperor in mind on all occasions . . . That'll be the day," he added under his breath. Moments later they were gone, disappearing into the rain which belted down in a solid sheet, as if it would never end again.

Grogan started to relax. The village had been evacuated, but not too rapidly. He could tell that by the interior of the little cottages. Hams had been cut from the rafters and all the traditional home-cured sausages had disappeared, as had the great plump feather beds upstairs. The villagers obviously had had time to take what they needed for their trek southwards. Even the fires in the tiled, roof-high stoves in the corner had gone out. He put his hand inside one and felt the ashes. They were stone cold: it had been hours since the fire had been extinguished. In the end he called off the house-to-house search and let his soaked exhausted teenagers take shelter. Shortly thereafter Mallory came limping in to announce, "The steeple's okay, Grogan. Someone obviously used it as an observation post. There are fag ends."

"Fag ends?" Grogan queried.

"Ends of cigarettes – everywhere. But they're cold. They've been out for ages."

"So, we won't lose our virginity this day," Grogan said happily, indicating his youngsters. "They're saved to die gloriously on yet another day."

Mallory nodded, but he could not altogether share the

American's obvious relief. He was still haunted by the feeling that they were being observed, that everything was not as "hunky-dory", to use Grogan's phrase, as it seemed to be. In essence, it appeared to Commander Mallory, the veteran of six years of war on three continents, that things were going *too damned well*.

One hundred yards away, Thaelmann and Spiv already knew that Mallory's hunch was right.

"Turds," Spiv said, staring at the steaming heap of dark brown horse manure, flecked with straw.

"Horse apples," Thaelmann agreed, using the German word, the rain streaming down through the branches where they had found the tell-tale pile of fresh horse droppings.

"Yes," Spiv responded, and pointed to the soaked grassfield beyond, "and whoever rode the nag – and it wasn't an old one either – took off in a hurry." He indicated the depressions in the wet grass, where the horse had placed its hooves. "Right smartish . . . Look at the distance between each pair of the nag's hooves."

Thaelmann nodded, shaking his head to dislodge the rain-drops dripping from the helmet rim on to his scarlet face before replying: "At the gallop. So what do you make of it, Spiv?"

Although the former cockney barrow boy, whose mind was normally concerned with two things – sex and profit – held no truck with Thaelmann's communist philosophy, he respected the former's quickness of mind.

"It was a Jerry . . . and he was watching us. You can see that from where he placed himself next to this tree to give him cover and allow him to watch the road coming into the village from the south."

"Agreed. And then?"

"And then?" Spiv repeated. "Whoever was watching us galloped off as soon as we got too close – and he was a loner, nothing to do with the rest of the folk in the village, who did a bunk carefully, taking their stuff with them as we've seen."

"Yes, Spiv," Thaelmann persisted. "But what was he going to do with what he'd learned?"

Spiv shrugged his shoulders his little ferret face showing his annoyance, for spivs such as he were never supposed to get caught out. "Search me, for frig's sake! What else do you think I can frigging well do – walk across the water like Jesus?"

was very large and they couldn't go on swanning about all over the show. They needed more precise information.

He sucked his teeth and didn't like the taste. He could have done with a drink, even if it was only water. He thrust back the thick feather covering and shivered in the suddenly cold air. Hastily he slipped on his boots unlaced and then, as an afterthought, he thrust his pistol in his waistbelt. After all, this was a combat zone, despite the seeming remoteness of the shooting war. As quietly as he could, he threaded his way through the snoring men in the darkness, heading for the kitchen and the handpump at the sink. He opened the door. The smell of *Camels* smoked by the paras had vanished, having been replaced by that of manure coming from the huge pile stored beneath the kitchen window, as was customary in rural Germany.

He pumped the squeaky, rusty apparatus a couple of times. The water stored in the well in the courtyard started to trickle out of the tap. Greedily, not waiting for his canteen to fill, he bent his head underneath and swallowed a "soss", as they used to call it as kids. It was then that he noticed the other smell, which, when he had entered the primitive kitchen, had been overpowered by that of the animal manure. It was one that he recognised immediately, that familiar combination of black coarse tobacco, garlic and sweat. It was the smell of the Hun!

Mallory straightened up abruptly, his thirst forgotten immediately. The smell was coming from outside, not from within the house. Besides, the occupants of the place had quit it hours, perhaps even days, before. No, that was the fresh odour of Germans – and they could only be the enemy, with evil intentions. Why else would they be outside in such weather at this time of the night? Besides, the Germans knew about the six o'clock evening curfew that the Allies had placed on all Germans in the areas under Allied control.

He straightened up and peered through the little window. There was nothing visible in the spectral light of the sickle moon sailing through the clouds at a great rate. He narrowed his eyes and peered from side to side carefully, in the approved fashion used by the military in achieving decent night vision. Again nothing, just the jagged outline of the old apple trees that the peasants used to make their *Apfelwein*.

He smiled to himself. "You're seeing things . . . imagining 'em," he whispered in the manner of lonely men who talk to themselves. The words died on his lips. Had he imagined away the sentry who had been posted outside the little HQ just before he and Grogan had turned in? As was customary with the Yanks, Grogan's young paras had had little training in night combat. They made too much noise, talked when being relieved and often smoked while on sentry, easily giving away their position. Now there was no sign of this particular sentry, and suddenly Mallory felt his heart begin to beat more rapidly. There was something up. He knew it. He felt it in his very bones. He had to act – but what was he supposed to do without making a great big fool of himself in front of the Yanks?

He took the pistol from his wristband and moved softly to the backdoor of the kitchen. Carefully, very carefully, he opened it, praying it wouldn't squeak like most of the doors in the old house. It didn't. The pre-dawn air was fresh and cold. He shivered a little. But he had no time to look for his tunic now. He stepped out, taking care where he placed his feet. All was silent. He crouched low and, pulling out his 45, he clicked off the safety catch. It seemed to make a hell of a lot of noise.

Cautiously he moved, still crouched low, towards the nearest tree. It would give him cover and at the same time make as good an observation post as anything else around. Suddenly he stopped short. There was someone standing there, a mere couple of feet away, propped against the tree, as if he, too, were watching out for whatever lay there.

Phew! Mallory breathed a sigh of relief after his first shocked reaction. Now he could recognise the typical round paratroop helmet that the silent figure was wearing. It was one of the Yank sentries, who had taken his orders very seriously, even to the extent of wearing his helmet. He pursed his abruptly very dry lips and called, "Hey, did you hear something as well?"

There was no answer.

It seemed the figure was too engrossed in his self-imposed task of watching the fields beyond. The Yank sentry did not even move at Mallory's voice.

Mallory moved forward a few paces. There was something wrong. The Yank had definitely spotted something. He reached out his left hand, grip damply tightening on the pistol in his right, "What is it—"

The words died on his lips.

Slowly but inevitably the sentry was beginning to keel over at the very same instant as Mallory touched him. "What—" he began.

Next moment the burst of MG 42 fire ripped along the length of the meadow and a green rain of new leaves came fluttering down as the German machine gun tore the apple orchard apart with its tremendous opening salvo.

Mallory ducked instinctively. At his feet the sentry lay crumpled, and in the momentary scarlet flash of gunfire Mallory caught a glimpse of the knife sticking out of the dead para's back. Even as everything went pitch-black again, he recognised the red and white diamond with the crooked cross of the swastika emblazoned on the dagger. It was the ceremonial dagger of the Hitler Youth. Next moment he had dismissed the questions raised in his mind and was pumping shots to left and right at a figure flitting from tree to tree. Behind him in the houses, yelled orders and sudden cries of alarm indicated that Grogan's youngsters were alerted too.

The muted firing in the distance roused von Dodenburg from an uneasy sleep. He had been dreaming about the future. It hadn't been rosy. He had been surrounded by hard-faced men in American helmets and uniforms, wearing sunglasses for some reason or other. They had been systematically stripping him of his badges of rank. Then had come his medals and orders, greedily snatched from his chest with chortles of glee and delight. His uniform had come next until he was completely naked, being jeered at, his genitals being poked at with sticks, by these Americans who towered above him so that he felt like some midget being toyed with by a bunch of giants.

He awoke with a start, feeling his body drenched with sweat. For one long moment he didn't know where he was. He shook his head hard. His vision cleared and he could make out the dim outlines of the men who had been sleeping on the floor all around him, beginning to grab for their boots and weapons. Only Hackmann seemed fully awake and dressed. He crouched at the blacked out window, peering out through a chink in the sacking curtain.

"Over here, *Obersturm*. Come and get a look." He beamed at von Dodenburg, as if he were pleased with himself for some reason or other.

Von Dodenburg followed his instruction. He bent next to Hackmann, who smelled nauseatingly of some cheap eau-de-Cologne or other. He peered out. On the horizon there was the sharp scarlet flame of a small arms fight. Tracer zipped through the air like a flight of angry hornets. Here and there came momentary bursts of flame and white smoke as grenades exploded. Even at that distance he could tell that the machine gun which kept hammering away was *Ami*. There was no mistaking that ponderous slow rate of fire from one of their World War One half-inch machine guns.

"What's going on? They're Americans out there. Are they firing at the Russkis?" von Dodenburg asked.

Carefully Hackmann lit a stump of candle and, cradling the flickering flame, placed the light between him and von Dodenburg, who was now wide awake. It was four o'clock in the morning. At zero six hundred hours, he'd stand the men to; they had a long day in front of them. They had to use the time, too, before those damned fat cats of *Ami* pilots finished their bacon and egg breakfasts and real bean coffee and came gunning for them. Thereafter their progress would be a slow cat and mouse game with the Allied "terror flyers".

"You know what *Werewolf* means?" Hackmann said carefully.

Kuno shrugged as if bored. In reality he wasn't, but for different reasons than Hackmann might have anticipated. "Yes, according to the old legend it's someone who could transform himself from man into wolf."

"Yes. *Reichsführer* Himmler was very interested in the concept. I did some research for him on the subject before I was transferred to Bormann's staff. It seems that in the Middle Ages people really believed in the concept. Men who were possessed of a great hatred of society had the power to transform themselves and make society pay for its supposed misdeeds."

"*Reichsführer* Himmler is crazy," Kuno said plainly, as a statement of fact. "He even believes in witches."

"Just so, just so," Hackmann responded evenly. "At that time there were German knights who put the concept to good use to get rid of their enemies without legal punishment. They used the werewolf concept to cover their own secret courts which pronounced sentence – illegally, naturally – and had that sentence carried out in the name of werewolf executions."

Kuno von Dodenburg nodded, interested now in spite of himself, as he sat there, his tough scarred face hollowed out to a death's head in the flickering yellow flame of the candle stub. "Some of our people did the same after the first war, when we were occupied by the Allies after we lost the battle," he interjected.

"*Genau*," Hackmann agreed, suddenly enthusiastic. "They murdered Allied control commission officers who were about to discover something they shouldn't have, and those disgusting German traitors who worked for them."

"And today?" Kuno beat Hackmann to his surprise announcement. "We have formed a similar organisation to deal with the new *Ami* control commission and our own self-seeking turncoats who work for them?"

"Exactly!" Hackmann confirmed excitedly.

For a moment von Dodenburg was preoccupied with a gory

vision of great hairy wolves, their huge claws dripping blood and their fang teeth with chunks of scarlet flesh hanging from them. He grinned at the thought before dismissing it with, "And who are these heroes going to be? Who will tackle the victorious Allies? What new bold knights are now prepared to spring into the breach and redress the balance?" He shrugged with mock, ironic modesty. "After all, we old hares with six years of combat experience behind us have patently failed the Reich."

Hackmann was in no mood for irony. "*Obersturmbann-führer* von Dodenburg," he snapped formally, "please don't joke about such matters. We have lost a battle but not the war."

Kuno was tempted to interject that they had also lost most of Germany, too, but thought better of it. Throughout the war he had met fanatics like Hackmann, who pontificated safely about battle from behind a desk in an office, seated on leather chairs, with pretty nubile secretaries bringing in coffee and cognac at regular intervals. Such people had no concept of real battle. Undoubtedly, when all the young men were long dead, they would pass away safely and gently in the comfort of their own beds – *from old age*.

"Who?" Hackmann asked rhetorically. "I shall tell you who. The brave young boys and girls of the Hitler Youth."

Kuno von Dodenburg looked at Hackmann's pudgy, bespectacled face, utterly aghast.

Three

The big girl in the white blouse and black skirt of the Association of German Maidens had been both skilled and lucky. But naturally, at sixteen she had had ten years of training behind her. She was as tough and dangerous as the boys who led the equivalent Hitler Youth. What was it they said they should all be? "As hard as Krupp steel, as tough as leather and as quick as a greyhound." She had been all of those, and when it was clear that their attack on the decadent *Ami* swine had failed, she had done what was expected of her – run for it. After all, had their instructors not always maintained that it was a leader's duty to live to fight another day? The weak would perish; the tough would survive.

The foolish kids had attempted to run back into the fields when the *Amis* had come out firing. It was as if they had wanted to sign their death warrant. How could they fight with their backs towards the enemy? The *Amis* had mown them down like dumb animals – a two-legged animal massacre. She had taken a different tack.

She had advanced straight down the village street, walking right in the middle of the unpaved road, clearly outlined by every explosion, making out that she was harmless and not an immediate threat to the young Americans firing wildly at their attackers. Indeed, once or twice they had shouted at her and she had guessed that they had wanted her to get out of the way of the crossfire, as if she had been some fool of a girl who had wandered into the battle by mistake. And all the time she had kept an egg grenade in her left hand, with the cotter pin drawn

115

so that it would explode as soon as she threw it, and an automatic in her right pocket.

It had worked until she had reached the outskirts of the embattled village and she had begun to relax. The *Ami* had stepped out of the shadows and caught her completely off guard. But she responded quicker than he had anticipated. She had flung the grenade wildly into the field behind him. The explosion had fooled him, and he had yelled something as the night darkness was split by the vivid jagged flame of the grenade exploding, turning instinctively. She didn't give him a chance, the automatic spitting fire and the slug catching him in the belly. He had gasped, as if he had been kicked by a mule. The impact had propelled him backwards, off his feet. He had slammed into the nearest tree and had hung there momentarily, before beginning to slide down the trunk slowly, dying as he did so. Moments later she had cleared the village and had been swallowed up into the darkness, presumably the sole survivor of the abortive *Werewolf* attack.

Now, as the sky started to flush an ugly dirty white, the first sign of dawn, she considered her position. There were German troops in the neighbourhood, she knew that from the signals from Berlin. But where there were German troops, she guessed, there'd be Russian, and she had already met the damned Americans. She had to be careful. She preferred the company of girls and didn't like men. But she knew all the same that men, whatever their nationality, were fools. All of them were basically concerned with that ugly dirty thing they had dangling between their legs. Their minds went blank when they encountered a woman. That was the trick she was going to play, if things went wrong. Exhausted but encouraged, she marched on.

Behind her the American convoy set off again on their penetration into the unknown. To mark their passing they left a ruined, still smoking hamlet, and those sad little fresh mounds of brown earth, topped by an upturned rifle surmounted by a helmet. It was the religious mark of a war-torn Europe, circa ten hundred hours, May 1st, 1945.

In the end the girl made her decision. She pulled out her pistol, checked that she still had a full magazine, unbuckled her belt and threw away the holster, then hitching up her dress, she stuck the little automatic in the back of her knickers. She looked to left and right. The countryside was deserted. But in the distance she could just make out another village, much like the ruined one which she had just left. Thin trails of curling blue smoke were coming from half a dozen places. The village was occupied and it had to have a post office. It would be a useful spot from where she could report to the *Zentrale*, using the network of post office telephones which the organisation had built since Christmas. And there was no time to be wasted. Wetting her dry lips, her pretty face set and determined, she set off. Things were moving again.

"You know what, Matzi?" Schulze said lazily as the heavily laden little convoy moved steadily down the country road, silent and empty as though the war were a million miles away.

Matz didn't raise his head. He was studying the dirty photograph he had taken off one of the dead Cossacks, who had obviously taken it in turn from some poor dead German stubblehopper, for it was a German postcard. It depicted a happy soldier who was wearing the *pickelhaube* of the Kaiser's army. On his back he had a heavy pack, obviously stuffed with goodies for his family. In front of him he pushed a barrow, on which reclined – there was no other word for it, Matz told himself – a huge swollen penis, like some great seal sunning itself on a rock. Underneath, the legend read "*Der Urlauber*" – "The Leaveman".

"You know what, Matzi?" Schulze repeated, a little louder the second time, a hint of menace in his voice, as they sunned themselves in the back of the littered halftrack.

"No, and I don't want to . . . but you'll frigging well tell me all the same," Matz finally responded. He studied the picture again. There was something very true about that dirty post-card, more wisdom than a score of clever books read by arsehole professors. That was what life was about for your ordinary common-or-garden, sent-to-the-front swine. A bit of knicky-knocky now and again, some good fodder and, naturally, plenty of Munich suds – and he was happy. It was all he was going to get anyhow—

"Are you listening to me, Corporal Matz?" Schulze snapped very formally, stung into words by the silence resulting from Matz's reverie. "That's the least bit of respect I can expect. After all I'm only the most senior sergeant here present."

"Boo hoo hoo," Matz wailed as he pretended to dab tears away from his eyes. "Don't break my heart, Sarnt Major. We all *do* love you."

"You'll have the toe of my frigging dice-breaker," by which he meant his jackboot, "up yer loving ass in half a mo, if you ain't careful. Now where was I?"

Matz shrugged and tucked away the dirty picture carefully inside his shabby grey tunic, remarking, "It'll help a bit when the five-fingered widow ain't too enthusiastic."

Schulze's face brightened. "That's it. Theme number one." He looked directly at his old running mate and declared, voice suddenly full of emotion, "Matzi, I hate to confess this, but . . . but" – he pulled himself together bravely, bottom lip quivering – "but I'm impotent. All the ink in my fountain pen has dried up and I won't be able to write to anybody anymore."

"That'd be the day."

"You're a shitting unfeeling horse's ass, aren't yer, Matzi?" Schulze retorted hotly. "What would you say if that happened to you? Though with the little bit of bacon you've got hanging between yer skinny shanks, you wouldn't notice, I suspect! But still, all the same, you'd want some sort of sympathy from an old pal, wouldn't yer?"

But Matz had no time to comment on the parlous state of his old friend's sex life, for before he could open his mouth, there was a volley of shots to their immediate front, and the noisy clatter of hooves coming down along the road at a gallop.

The two old hares shot upwards immediately, already